1

This book belongs to:

_____

Cancer Daily Horoscope 2026

Author's Note: Time set to EDT and EST Zone (UTC-4, UTC-5)

Mystic Cat
Suite 41906, 3/2237 Gold Coast HWY
Mermaid Beach, Queensland, 4218
Australia
islandauthor@hotmail.com

Contents

The 12 Zodiac Star Signs

2026

January

S	M	T	W	T	F	S
				1	2	3
4	5	6	7	8	9	10
11	12	13	14	15	16	17
18	19	20	21	22	23	24
25	26	27	28	29	30	31

February

S	M	T	W	T	F	S
1	2	3	4	5	6	7
8	9	10	11	12	13	14
15	16	17	18	19	20	21
22	23	24	25	26	27	28

March

S	M	T	W	T	F	S
1	2	3	4	5	6	7
8	9	10	11	12	13	14
15	16	17	18	19	20	21
22	23	24	25	26	27	28
29	30	31				

April

S	M	T	W	T	F	S
			1	2	3	4
5	6	7	8	9	10	11
12	13	14	15	16	17	18
19	20	21	22	23	24	25
26	27	28	29	30		

May

S	M	T	W	T	F	S
					1	2
3	4	5	6	7	8	9
10	11	12	13	14	15	16
17	18	19	20	21	22	23
24	25	26	27	28	29	30
31						

June

S	M	T	W	T	F	S
	1	2	3	4	5	6
7	8	9	10	11	12	13
14	15	16	17	18	19	20
21	22	23	24	25	26	27
28	29	30				

July

S	M	T	W	T	F	S
			1	2	3	4
5	6	7	8	9	10	11
12	13	14	15	16	17	18
19	20	21	22	23	24	25
26	27	28	29	30	31	

August

S	M	T	W	T	F	S
						1
2	3	4	5	6	7	8
9	10	11	12	13	14	15
16	17	18	19	20	21	22
23	24	25	26	27	28	29
30	31					

September

S	M	T	W	T	F	S
		1	2	3	4	5
6	7	8	9	10	11	12
13	14	15	16	17	18	19
20	21	22	23	24	25	26
27	28	29	30			

October

S	M	T	W	T	F	S
				1	2	3
4	5	6	7	8	9	10
11	12	13	14	15	16	17
18	19	20	21	22	23	24
25	26	27	28	29	30	31

November

S	M	T	W	T	F	S
1	2	3	4	5	6	7
8	9	10	11	12	13	14
15	16	17	18	19	20	21
22	23	24	25	26	27	28
29	30					

December

S	M	T	W	T	F	S
		1	2	3	4	5
6	7	8	9	10	11	12
13	14	15	16	17	18	19
20	21	22	23	24	25	26
27	28	29	30	31		

Cancer Daily Horoscope
2026

The time zone is America Eastern Time,
EST or EDT during daylight saving time.
The GMT offset is -5:00.

In the realm of astrology, the differences between various horoscope books for each zodiac sign stem from the intricate tapestry of celestial activity constantly unfolding in the skies. As your astrologer, my approach is to hone in on the pivotal aspects affecting a specific star sign on any given day, recognizing the uniqueness inherent in each zodiac entity.

Crafting horoscopes demands a discerning focus on the predominant astrological influences directly shaping the experiences of a particular sign. While multiple planetary configurations may be at play, I prioritize the astrological aspects that carry greater significance for a specific zodiac sign.

Delving into the ruling planets, houses, and elemental attributes associated with each sign further enriches the depth of my interpretations. This meticulous attention ensures that the guidance provided resonates authentically with the distinctive characteristics and tendencies of the intended audience.

The objective is to deliver personalized insights and advice grounded in the cosmic dynamics relevant to each zodiac sign. By emphasizing the most impactful astrological facets, I aim to assist readers in comprehending themselves more profoundly and navigating the energies surrounding them. By embracing the strengths, challenges, and opportunities inherent in each zodiac sign, my horoscope book endeavors to offer a tailored and insightful roadmap for self-discovery and growth.

Crystal

"The starry vault of heaven is in truth the open book of cosmic projection…"

—Carl Jung

JANUARY

Mon	Tue	Wed	Thu	Fri	Sat	Sun
			1	2	3	4
5	6	7	8	9	10	11
12	13	14	15	16	17	18
19	20	21	22	23	24	25
26	27	28	29	30	31	

NEW MOON

_____

_____

_____

_____

_____

_____

_____

_____

_____

_____

_____

_____

_____

_____

_____

_____

_____

_____

Wolf Moon

29 Monday

As the Moon gracefully enters Taurus, you may notice a shift to a more grounded and stable emotional state. This astrological transition encourages you to seek comfort, security, and a connection to the physical world. Taurus' energy fosters a desire for simplicity, indulgence in life's pleasures, and a sense of appreciation for the material aspects of life. During this time, you might find solace in enjoying good food, embracing creature comforts, or spending time in nature.

30 Tuesday

When Mercury squares Saturn, you may face communication challenges and mental hurdles. Your thoughts and ideas may clash with the practical, disciplined approach Saturn encourages. It can feel like your mind is weighed down by self-doubt and a sense of limitation, making it difficult to express yourself confidently. This aspect can lead to a tendency to overthink or be overly critical of your words and actions.

31 Wednesday

Moon ingress Gemini lunar shift can infuse your celebrations with light-hearted and communicative energy, making it an ideal time for connecting with friends and loved ones. You might engage in lively conversations, share stories, and embrace a more adaptable and curious mindset. It's an opportunity to ring in the new year with intellectual curiosity and playfulness as you seek new experiences and connections that keep the festivities vibrant and engaging.

1 Thursday

At 4:12 PM, Mercury ingresses into Capricorn, marking a shift in the way thoughts and communication are expressed. Capricorn's influence brings a more practical, disciplined, and goal-oriented approach to thinking and speaking. This transit encourages strategic planning, organization, and a focus on long-term goals in communication. It's a favorable time for structured discussions, serious conversations, and practical decision-making.

2 Friday

The Moon ingresses into Cancer, emphasizing emotional sensitivity, nurturing instincts, and a desire for security. Cancer is the sign ruled by the Moon, so its ingress enhances your emotional receptivity and heightens your need for comfort and familiarity. During this lunar transit, you may find yourself more attuned to the needs of loved ones and seeking solace in domestic activities. Creating a cozy and nurturing environment becomes a priority.

3 Saturday

The Full Moon illuminates the skies, marking a significant moment of culmination and completion. Full Moons are times of heightened emotions and awareness, bringing matters to fruition and shedding light on areas that require attention or release. It's a powerful time for manifestation, closure, and letting go. Please pay attention to any insights or revelations that arise during this potent lunar phase, as they may guide greater clarity and alignment with your intentions.

4 Sunday

At 8:43 AM, the Moon ingresses into Leo, infusing the atmosphere with warmth, vitality, and creativity. With the Moon in Leo, emotions become more dramatic and expressive, and there's a desire for recognition, appreciation, and self-expression. This lunar transit encourages you to embrace your passions, shine brightly, and share your unique gifts. It's a time to indulge in activities that bring you joy and fulfillment, as well as to nurture your inner fire and confidence.

5 Monday

Sun in Capricorn in the seventh house enhances your ability to manage your relationships with confidence and strategic insight. You may feel more driven to achieve harmony and success in your partnerships through disciplined and well-organized efforts. Embrace this opportunity to refine your relationship dynamics, creating connections that are both supportive and enduring. Your practical approach to relationships helps you address conflicts and build a solid foundation.

6 Tuesday

Under the influence of today's Virgo moon, emotions may be processed through a lens of practicality and pragmatism. You may find satisfaction in attending to chores, organizing your environment, and refining your routines. This transit is a favorable time for making improvements in your habits, diet, and overall well-being. Harness the diligent energy of Virgo to streamline your daily tasks and address any areas that require attention to detail.

7 Wednesday

With Mercury in Capricorn transiting your seventh house, your approach to relationships and partnerships becomes more strategic and practical. This period encourages you to communicate with clarity and purpose, focusing on building solid and stable connections. You may find yourself more willing to engage in discussions that require careful planning and negotiation. It is a time to channel your mental energy into creating harmonious and well-structured partnerships.

8 Thursday

At 7:07 AM, as Mercury forms a sextile with the North Node, it presents you with an opportunity to align your thoughts and communication with your life's purpose. This aspect encourages you to express yourself authentically and in a way that resonates with your soul's evolution. You may find that your ideas and conversations naturally guide you toward personal growth and fulfillment. You can embrace this energy to navigate conversations with confidence and clarity.

9 Friday

At 12:34 PM, Venus opposes Jupiter, creating a dynamic interplay between love, abundance, and expansion in your life. This aspect highlights a tension between your desires for pleasure, indulgence, and growth. You may feel a strong urge to pursue opportunities for enjoyment, whether in relationships, finances, or creative endeavors. However, there's a risk of overindulgence or extravagance under this influence, as Jupiter's influence tends to magnify whatever it touches.

10 Saturday

At 3:42 AM, the Sun opposes Jupiter, creating a dynamic tension between your ego and your sense of expansion and growth. This aspect can bring about a clash between your desire for success, recognition, and abundance and the need for moderation and realism. You may feel inclined to take risks or overextend yourself. Strive to find a balance between confidence and humility and avoid making impulsive decisions based solely on optimism.

11 Sunday

The Moon gracefully transitions into Scorpio, infusing your emotions with intensity, depth, and a desire for transformation. During this lunar transit, you may find yourself delving into the mysteries of life, probing beneath the surface to uncover hidden truths. Emotions run deep under Scorpio's influence, encouraging you to explore your innermost desires, fears, and passions. Use this time to embrace the power of emotional regeneration and embrace personal growth.

12 Monday

Mercury in Capricorn in the seventh house enhances your ability to negotiate and collaborate with confidence and professionalism. You may feel more driven to achieve mutual goals within your partnerships, setting clear objectives and developing structured plans to reach them. It is a time to approach your relationships with a practical and focused mindset. Your ability to articulate your ideas and manage your partnerships wisely can lead to significant progress.

13 Tuesday

At 6:34 PM, the Moon gracefully transitions into Sagittarius, heralding a time of exploration, expansion, and philosophical pursuits. As the Moon moves through this adventurous and optimistic sign, you may feel a strong urge to break free from routine, seek out new experiences, and broaden your horizons. Sagittarius encourages you to embrace spontaneity, embrace diversity, and cultivate a sense of wonder and curiosity about the world around you.

14 Wednesday

Mercury opposes Jupiter, creating a dynamic tension between communication, intellect, and expansion. This aspect may bring about a clash between optimism and practicality in your thoughts and conversations. On one hand, Jupiter's influence can inspire grand ideas, expansive thinking, and a desire for growth and abundance. However, when opposed by Mercury, there's a risk of overconfidence. Be mindful of the tendency to make promises or commitments that are unrealistic.

15 Thursday

Venus trines Uranus, infusing your interactions and experiences with excitement, spontaneity, and innovation. This aspect encourages you to embrace change, explore new possibilities, and break free from routine or stagnation in your relationships and artistic pursuits. You may feel inspired to experiment with unconventional ideas or seek out unique experiences. Embrace the unexpected and allow yourself to embrace the magic of spontaneity and discovery.

16 Friday

At 6:47 AM, the Moon gracefully transitions into Capricorn, marking a time of increased focus, determination, and practicality. During this lunar transition, you may find yourself drawn towards responsibilities, goals, and long-term plans. Capricorn's influence encourages you to approach tasks with discipline, efficiency, and a strong sense of ambition. Use this time to prioritize your responsibilities, organize your life, and pursue your aspirations with diligence.

17 Saturday

The Sun trines Uranus, bringing excitement, innovation, and unexpected opportunities for growth. This aspect encourages you to embrace change, break free from old patterns, and embrace your authentic self-expression. You may feel inspired to explore new ideas, take risks, and welcome positive changes that lead to greater freedom and liberation. Trust in your intuition, embrace spontaneity, and be open to the thrilling possibilities that emerge during this electrifying transit.

18 Sunday

At 2:53 PM, a New Moon graces the sky, marking a potent time for new beginnings, fresh intentions, and planting seeds for the future. This lunar phase invites you to set clear intentions, envision your goals, and embark on a journey of self-discovery and manifestation. Embrace the energy of renewal and possibilities as you align your actions with your deepest desires, paving the way for growth and transformation in the lunar cycle ahead.

19 Monday

Mercury forms a harmonious trine with Uranus, igniting your intellect with innovative ideas, sudden insights, and flashes of inspiration. This aspect encourages you to think outside the box, embrace change, and explore unconventional solutions to problems. Allow your mind to break free from routine and tap into the brilliance of your unique perspective. Embrace the excitement of exploration and trust in your ability to adapt to new situations with ease.

20 Tuesday

Mercury's ingress into Aquarius initiates a period of innovative thinking and intellectual exploration. During this transition, your mind is attuned to progressive ideas, social causes, and unconventional perspectives. Embrace your role as a visionary thinker, advocate for change, and engage in meaningful conversations that contribute to progress and enlightenment. Embrace your unique perspective as you contribute to the collective tapestry of ideas.

21 Wednesday

The Moon in Pisces infuses the atmosphere with sensitivity, intuition, and a deep connection to the unseen realms. During this lunar transit, you may find yourself more attuned to your emotions and the subtle energies that surround you. Pisces' influence encourages you to embrace compassion, creativity, and spiritual exploration. Allow yourself to flow with the gentle currents of intuition and imagination, trusting in the wisdom of your inner guidance.

22 Thursday

Mercury in Aquarius in the eighth house enhances your ability to handle intimacy and shared resources with innovation and determination. You may feel more driven to achieve shared goals through clear and well-organized efforts. It is a time to approach your intimate relationships and financial matters with a progressive and systematic mindset, allowing your attention to new ideas to bring about significant growth.

23 Friday

At 1:39 AM, Mars sextiles Neptune, infusing your actions with creativity, intuition, and spiritual insight. This aspect encourages you to channel your energy into pursuits that align with your higher ideals and innermost dreams. Embrace the synergy between ambition and imagination, allowing inspiration to guide your endeavors toward meaningful expression and fulfillment. Trust in the power of intuition to lead you towards inspired action.

24 Saturday

As Venus moves through Aquarius in your eighth house, you may feel a stronger desire to delve into the mysteries of life and explore esoteric or metaphysical subjects. This transit can deepen your understanding of the unseen forces that influence your life, fostering a sense of spiritual awakening and transformation. Embrace the opportunity to explore these deeper realms, allowing them to guide you toward greater self-awareness and personal growth.

25 Sunday

At 11:48 PM, the Moon reaches its first quarter phase, marking a pivotal moment in the lunar cycle for decision-making and taking action. This lunar phase encourages you to assess your progress, overcome obstacles, and make adjustments to your plans as needed. Embrace the dynamic energy of the first Quarter Moon to step into your power, assert your intentions, and move forward with confidence and determination.

26 Monday

At 2:16 PM, Neptune gracefully transitions into Aries, marking a significant shift in the collective consciousness towards innovation, independence, and pioneering spirit. During this transit, the dreamy and mystical energy of Neptune combines with the bold and assertive qualities of Aries, inspiring you to pursue your dreams with courage and conviction. Embrace the call to embark on new adventures, explore uncharted territories, and tap into your inner fire to manifest your visions.

27 Tuesday

At 3:55 PM, the Moon gracefully transitions into Gemini, infusing the atmosphere with curiosity, versatility, and sociability. During this lunar transition, your mind becomes more agile and adaptable, and you may find yourself eager to engage in conversation, gather information, and explore new ideas. Embrace the light-hearted energy of Gemini to stimulate your intellect, connect with others through meaningful communication, and pursue a variety of interests with enthusiasm.

28 Wednesday

Sun in Aquarius in the Eighth House enhances your ability to navigate the depths of your psyche with creativity and insight. You may feel more driven to explore the unknown and confront your fears with courage and curiosity. Embrace this opportunity to delve into your subconscious mind and uncover hidden motivations and desires. Your innovative approach to personal growth will help you break free from limiting beliefs and transform your life in powerful ways.

29 Thursday

At 5:31 PM, the Moon tenderly transitions into Cancer, enveloping you in a nurturing and emotional embrace. During this lunar transit, you may find yourself drawn to the comforts of home, family, and close relationships. Cancer's influence encourages you to prioritize emotional security, connect with your innermost feelings, and nurture both yourself and those you care about. Embrace the gentle waves of Cancerian energy to create a haven for yourself.

FEBRUARY

Mon	Tue	Wed	Thu	Fri	Sat	Sun
						1
2	3	4	5	6	7	8
9	10	11	12	13	14	15
16	17	18	19	20	21	22
23	24	25	26	27	28	

NEW MOON

_____

_____

_____

_____

_____

_____

_____

_____

_____

_____

_____

_____

_____

_____

_____

_____

_____

_____

_____

SNOW MOON

_____

_____

_____

_____

_____

_____

_____

_____

_____

_____

_____

_____

_____

_____

_____

_____

_____

_____

_____

_____

_____

_____

_____

30 Friday

With Mars in Aquarius transiting your eighth house, your approach to intimacy and shared resources becomes more adventurous and unconventional. You are likely to seek deeper connections that challenge and transform you, embracing experiences that push the limits of your comfort zone. This period encourages you to explore new dimensions of emotional and physical intimacy. Dive into the transformative power of vulnerability, allowing it to strengthen your bonds.

31 Saturday

At 7:09 PM, the Moon majestically enters Leo, infusing the atmosphere with warmth, vitality, and expressive energy. During this lunar transit, you may feel a heightened sense of confidence, creativity, and desire for recognition. Leo's influence encourages you to shine brightly, express yourself authentically, and embrace your unique gifts and talents. Embrace the spotlight with grace and enthusiasm, allowing your inner light to illuminate the world around you.

1 Sunday

At 5:10 PM, the Full Moon illuminates the sky, marking a powerful culmination with heightened emotions. This lunar phase symbolizes clarity, completion, and the fulfillment of intentions set during the New Moon. As the Moon reaches its peak in illumination, emotions may run high, and insights may surface with greater clarity. It's a time to celebrate achievements, release what no longer serves you, and express gratitude for the blessings in your life.

2 Monday

The Moon gracefully transitions into Virgo, bringing a shift towards practicality. During this lunar transit, you may feel inclined to focus on productivity, health, and self-improvement efforts. Virgo's influence encourages you to analyze situations critically, refine your routines, and strive for greater efficiency in your daily life. Embrace Virgo's diligent energy in attending to tasks with precision, cultivating order, and working towards achieving your goals with dedication.

3 Tuesday

Uranus now moves forward, encouraging you to embrace your individuality, break free from limitations, and pursue your unique path with courage and authenticity. This planetary shift may bring sudden insights, breakthroughs, and opportunities for revolutionary change in your life. Embrace the electrifying energy of Uranus as you embark on a journey of self-discovery, liberation, and creative evolution.

4 Wednesday

A compelling journey ahead draws remarkable results, allowing you to gain traction in developing your dreams. It corresponds with planning, gathering intel, and having all the resources required to advance life. Increased Aquarian activity stakes your claim in an ambitious area that captures the essence of excitement. It makes you feel optimistic about possibilities, giving you the green light. Watch for signs as important clues reveal unique opportunities meant for your life.

5 Thursday

Mercury squares Uranus, creating a dynamic tension between intellect and innovation. This aspect may lead to sudden insights, brilliant ideas, and unexpected changes in communication. You may find yourself feeling restless, eager for mental stimulation, and open to exploring new perspectives. However, be mindful of the tendency towards impulsiveness or rebelliousness. Strive to stay flexible and adapt to unexpected developments with curiosity and an open mind.

6 Friday

Mercury gracefully transitions into Pisces, infusing the atmosphere with a dreamy, imaginative, and intuitive energy. During this transit, your thoughts and communications may become more influenced by emotions, intuition, and spiritual insights. Pisces' influence encourages you to tap into your subconscious mind, embrace creativity, and express yourself with compassion and empathy. You may find yourself more drawn to acts of kindness and understanding.

7 Saturday

At 2:13 PM, the Moon gracefully transitions into Scorpio, infusing the atmosphere with intensity, depth, and emotional transformation. During this lunar transit, you may feel drawn to explore the mysteries of life, delve into the realms of the subconscious, and confront hidden truths within yourself and others. Scorpio's influence encourages you to embrace your inner power, release what no longer serves you, and undergo profound personal growth.

8 Sunday

At 4:48 AM, Venus squares Uranus, igniting a surge of excitement, unpredictability, and change in matters of love, relationships, and finances. This aspect may bring sudden shifts, unexpected events, or disruptions in your personal connections or financial situations. You may feel inclined to break free from routines, embrace your independence, or seek out unconventional experiences in your relationships or monetary matters.

9 Monday

At 7:44 AM, the Moon enters its last Quarter phase, marking a pivotal moment in the lunar cycle for reflection, release, and reassessment. This phase invites you to review your goals, evaluate your progress, and make any necessary adjustments as you prepare for the upcoming lunar cycle. It's a time to let go of what no longer serves you, release any attachments or burdens weighing you down, and clear the path for new beginnings.

10 Tuesday

The Moon gracefully transitions into Sagittarius, infusing the atmosphere with a sense of adventure, optimism, and expansion. During this lunar transit, you may feel a strong desire for exploration, learning, and freedom. Sagittarius' influence encourages you to embrace new experiences, broaden your horizons, and seek out opportunities for growth and discovery. Embrace the adventurous spirit of Sagittarius as you embark on a journey of self-discovery and cultural exploration.

11 Wednesday

Under the influence of today's energies, you may feel a strong desire to express your individuality, assert your independence, and pursue your goals with a sense of adventure. Use this energy to channel your passions into projects that excite you, explore unconventional ideas, and take calculated risks that lead to exciting opportunities for growth and expansion. Allow your intuition to guide you as you navigate uncharted territory and embrace the unexpected twists and turns.

12 Thursday

At 2:44 PM, the Moon gracefully transitions into Capricorn, infusing the atmosphere with a sense of determination, practicality, and responsibility. During this lunar transition, you may feel inclined to focus on your long-term goals, career aspirations, and the practical steps needed to achieve success. Capricorn's influence encourages you to take a disciplined approach to your tasks, prioritize your responsibilities, and strive for excellence in all your endeavors.

13 Friday

Saturn gracefully transitions into Aries, marking a significant shift in the cosmic landscape and a new chapter in collective responsibility and discipline. As Saturn, the planet of structure and authority, enters the fiery and assertive sign of Aries, themes of self-reliance, initiative, and independence come to the forefront. This transit encourages you to take ownership of your actions, assert your individuality, and cultivate a strong sense of self-discipline and determination.

14 Saturday

Mars's influence in Aquarius adds a significant touch of excitement and adventure to Valentine's Day. Known for its fiery and assertive energy, Mars in Aquarius ignites a passion for exploration and experimentation in matters of love. Couples may find themselves feeling more spontaneous and open to trying new things together. Singles may feel a surge of confidence to pursue their romantic interests and take bold leaps of faith.

15 Sunday

The Moon in Aquarius infuses the atmosphere with innovation, humanitarianism, and a spirit of individuality. During this lunar transition, you may feel a strong desire for freedom, progressive thinking, and social connection. Aquarius' influence encourages you to embrace your uniqueness, celebrate diversity, and contribute to collective endeavors that promote positive change. You may seek out new ideas, engage in conversations, and champion causes.

16 Monday

Mercury forms a harmonious trine aspect with Jupiter, enhancing communication, optimism, and intellectual growth. This aspect encourages expansive thinking, positive outlooks, and the exchange of ideas on a grand scale. You may feel more open-minded, enthusiastic, and eager to learn and share knowledge with others. Use this favorable energy to pursue opportunities for learning and travel and broaden your horizons through exploration.

17 Tuesday

Venus opposes the South Node, creating tension between relationships, values, and past patterns or karma. This aspect may bring up old dynamics in relationships that need to be addressed. It's a time to reflect on any unhealthy patterns or attachments in your relationships and to let go of anything that no longer serves your highest good. Break from limiting beliefs or behaviors in matters of love, self-worth, and pleasure to create healthier, fulfilling connections.

18 Wednesday

As the Sun moves through the mystical waters of Pisces, you may find yourself drawn to introspection, creativity, and connecting with the unseen realms. This transit invites you to embrace your imagination, cultivate compassion, and deepen your connection to the divine. Embrace the fluid and empathetic energy of Pisces as you explore your dreams, express your deepest emotions, and surrender to the flow of life's mysteries.

19 Thursday

At 2:39 PM, the Moon gracefully transitions into Aries, infusing the atmosphere with vitality, courage, and a pioneering spirit. During this lunar transit, you may feel a surge of energy and a desire to take action, assert your independence, and pursue your goals with enthusiasm. Aries' influence encourages you to embrace your inner warrior, embrace new beginnings, and fearlessly venture into uncharted territory.

20 Friday

Neptune in Aries in the tenth house enhances your ability to pursue career goals that resonate with your higher values and aspirations. You may feel more inspired to take on roles that allow you to express your creativity and make a positive difference. It is a time to trust your instincts and pursue paths that align with your true calling. Your ability to inspire and uplift others can lead to significant achievements and recognition.

21 Saturday

At 6:31 PM, the Moon gracefully transitions into Taurus, bringing a sense of stability, comfort, and groundedness to the atmosphere. During this lunar transit, you may feel inclined to prioritize security, indulge in sensual pleasures, and create a sense of abundance in your surroundings. Taurus' influence encourages you to slow down, savor the present moment, and cultivate a deeper appreciation for the beauty and richness of life.

22 Sunday

At 3:01 PM, Venus forms a harmonious trine aspect with Jupiter, creating an expansive and uplifting energy in matters of love, abundance, and pleasure. This aspect brings blessings, opportunities, and a sense of optimism in relationships, finances, and creative pursuits. You may feel more generous, open-hearted, and inclined to indulge in life's luxuries. It's a favorable time for socializing, enjoying cultural experiences, and connecting with others on a deeper level.

23 Monday

At 9:29 PM, the Moon gracefully transitions into Gemini, infusing the atmosphere with curiosity, versatility, and a desire for intellectual stimulation. During this lunar transit, you may feel more friendly, communicative, and eager to explore new ideas and perspectives. Gemini's influence encourages you to engage in lively conversations, exchange thoughts and information, and embrace variety in your experiences.

24 Tuesday

At 7:28 AM, the Moon reaches its First Quarter phase, which marks a significant milestone in the lunar cycle. This phase signifies a time of action, decision-making, and moving forward with your intentions set at the New Moon. It's a period of growth, challenges, and opportunities to overcome obstacles on your path. As the Moon squares the Sun, you may feel a push to take decisive action and make necessary adjustments to your plans.

25 Wednesday

Venus in Pisces in the ninth house enhances your ability to pursue academic and philosophical endeavors with grace and charm. You may feel more driven to achieve long-term educational and travel goals through meaningful and empathetic interactions. This is a time to approach your studies and explorations with a balanced and intuitive mindset. Your ability to communicate your ideas with compassion and creativity can lead to significant progress.

26 Thursday

At 1:47 AM, Mercury turns retrograde, marking a period of introspection, reflection, and revision in communication and mental processes. During this retrograde phase, you may encounter challenges in communication, technology, and decision-making. It's a time to review plans, reassess your thoughts and ideas, and resolve any lingering issues from the past. Embrace the opportunity to slow down, reevaluate your priorities, and gain insights from past experiences.

MARCH

Mon	Tue	Wed	Thu	Fri	Sat	Sun
						1
2	3	4	5	6	7	8
9	10	11	12	13	14	15
16	17	18	19	20	21	22
23	24	25	26	27	28	29
30	31					

NEW MOON

WORM MOON

_____

_____

_____

_____

_____

_____

_____

_____

_____

_____

_____

_____

_____

_____

_____

_____

_____

_____

_____

27 Friday

Mars squares Uranus, igniting a surge of unpredictable energy and potential disruptions in action and assertiveness. This aspect may bring sudden changes, impulsive behavior, or unexpected events that challenge your plans or goals. It's essential to remain flexible and adaptable in the face of uncertainty, as hasty actions or reckless behavior could lead to accidents or conflicts. Use this dynamic energy to channel your passions and desires into constructive outlets.

28 Saturday

At 3:17 AM, the Moon majestically transitions into Leo, infusing the atmosphere with confidence, creativity, and a desire for self-expression. During this lunar transit, you may feel more outgoing, enthusiastic, and inclined towards seeking attention and recognition. Leo's influence encourages you to embrace your unique talents, showcase your creativity, and express yourself authentically. It's a time for embracing your inner light, shining brightly, and sharing your gifts with the world.

1 Sunday

With the Sun in Pisces transiting your ninth house, your focus on higher learning and spiritual growth becomes more intuitive and empathetic. This period encourages you to approach your quest for knowledge and understanding with a sense of openness. You may find yourself more interested in exploring new philosophies, spiritual practices, and cultural experiences that expand your horizons. This is a time to channel your energy into seeking new opportunities.

2 Monday

At 9:19 AM, Mars enters Pisces, marking a shift towards compassion, intuition, and spiritual action. During this transition, your energy may become more diffuse, and you may find yourself motivated by ideals, dreams, and the desire to help others. Mars in Pisces encourages you to channel your assertiveness and drive into creative pursuits, spiritual practices, and acts of kindness and service. The energy of Pisces lets you navigate your desires and motivations with sensitivity and grace.

3 Tuesday

As the Moon reaches its peak in brightness, it invites you to reflect on your intentions set during the New Moon and acknowledge the progress you've made since then. Embrace the illuminating energy of the Full Moon to let go of what no longer serves you, celebrate your achievements, and embrace the transformative power of surrender. Allow the moonlight to guide you as you navigate the currents of change and move forward with a renewed sense of purpose and direction.

4 Wednesday

Venus forms a harmonious sextile aspect with Uranus, infusing the day with excitement, spontaneity, and opportunities for new experiences in love and creativity. You may feel a surge of creativity and originality, making it an ideal time to express yourself in unique ways or pursue exciting social encounters. Embrace the electrifying energy of Venus sextile Uranus to welcome unexpected delights and spark positive transformations.

5 Thursday

At 12:13 PM, the Sun forms a harmonious trine aspect with Jupiter, illuminating your path with optimism, abundance, and expansion. This cosmic alignment encourages you to embrace opportunities for growth, pursue your goals with confidence, and tap into your inner wisdom and potential. With the Sun's radiant energy combined with Jupiter's expansive influence, you may feel a surge of enthusiasm, optimism, and a sense of possibility.

6 Friday

At 11:01 PM, the Moon transitions into Scorpio, infusing the atmosphere with intensity, depth, and emotional transformation. During this lunar transit, you may find yourself delving into the realms of the subconscious, seeking more profound truths, and exploring hidden aspects of yourself and others. Scorpio's influence encourages you to embrace authenticity, confront your fears, and embrace the power of regeneration and rebirth.

7 Saturday

Mars in Pisces in the ninth house enhances your ability to pursue intellectual and spiritual growth with creativity and intuition. You may feel more driven to achieve educational and philosophical goals through compassionate and imaginative efforts. This is a time to approach your studies and travels with a flexible and empathetic mindset. Your ability to engage with complex ideas and embrace diverse cultures can lead to significant personal growth.

8 Sunday

Sun in Pisces in the ninth house enhances your ability to embrace new ideas and perspectives with an open heart and mind. You may feel more driven to explore new ways of connecting with the divine and understanding the mysteries of life. Embrace this opportunity to broaden your horizons and seek out experiences that inspire and enlighten you. Your compassionate approach to learning will help you connect with others on a deeper level and foster a sense of global unity.

9 Monday

At 11:36 AM, the Moon transitions into Sagittarius, infusing the atmosphere with a sense of adventure, optimism, and exploration. During this lunar transition, you may feel a strong desire for freedom, expansion, and philosophical understanding. Sagittarius' influence encourages you to embrace new experiences, broaden your horizons, and seek meaning in the world around you. It's a favorable time for travel, higher learning, and embracing the unknown with open arms.

10 Tuesday

At 11:36 PM, Jupiter turns direct after a period of retrograde motion, marking a significant shift in the realm of expansion, abundance, and opportunity. With Jupiter now moving forward again, its influence on growth, prosperity, and optimism becomes more pronounced. This planetary shift brings a renewed sense of hope, enthusiasm, and forward momentum, making it an ideal time to pursue your goals, broaden your horizons, and embrace new possibilities.

11 Wednesday

The Moon reaches its Last Quarter phase, marking a pivotal moment in the lunar cycle for reflection, release, and reassessment. This celestial event signals a time of culmination and completion, where you are encouraged to review your progress, let go of what no longer serves you, and prepare for the upcoming cycle of renewal. It's a potent opportunity to release old habits, beliefs, or situations that are holding you back and make space for new growth and possibilities.

12 Thursday

At 12:07 AM, the Moon gracefully transitions into Capricorn, marking a shift towards a more grounded, disciplined, and ambitious energy. During this lunar transition, you may feel a stronger sense of responsibility, determination, and focus on your long-term goals. Capricorn's influence encourages you to prioritize practicality, organization, and perseverance in your endeavors. It's a favorable time for setting goals and working diligently toward success.

13 Friday

At 4:52 PM, Mars forms an opposition with the South Node, creating a dynamic tension between your current actions and past karmic influences. This aspect may bring up old patterns, conflicts, or unresolved issues that need to be addressed and released. Use this opportunity to reflect on any self-limiting behaviors or outdated beliefs that may be holding you back and take decisive action to break free from old patterns and move forward with greater clarity and purpose.

14 Saturday

The Moon transitions into Aquarius, infusing the atmosphere with a sense of innovation, individuality, and humanitarianism. During this lunar transition, you may feel a stronger urge to express your unique perspective, embrace your eccentricities, and connect with like-minded individuals who share your ideals and values. Aquarius' influence encourages you to think outside the box, explore unconventional ideas, and contribute to collective causes for the greater good.

15 Sunday

As you head down the river of life, there will always be a few riverbed rocks that create turbulence. Learning how to navigate downstream towards calmer waters helps grow your experience. This cosmic influence brings skills and abilities that enable you to balance life's ups and downs without becoming adrift. Your willingness to expand horizons and set sail on new adventures brings a pleasing result. The stars guide your journey towards balance and adventure.

16 Monday

At 7:15 PM, the Moon gracefully transitions into Pisces, infusing the atmosphere with sensitivity, intuition, and empathy. During this lunar transit, you may feel more attuned to your emotions, dreams, and the subtle energies that permeate the world. Pisces' influence encourages you to embrace your imagination, creativity, and spiritual connection. It's a favorable time for introspection, meditation, and connecting with your innermost feelings.

17 Tuesday

At 5:00 PM, Mercury forms an opposition aspect with the South Node, creating a dynamic tension between your current thoughts and communication style and past influences or patterns. This aspect may bring up issues or conflicts related to outdated beliefs, habits, or ways of thinking that are no longer serving your highest good. You may find yourself facing challenges in expressing yourself effectively or encountering misunderstandings in communication.

18 Wednesday

At 12:08 PM, Venus forms a challenging square aspect with Jupiter, creating tension between love, pleasure, and expansion. This aspect may bring about excessiveness or overindulgence in relationships, finances, or enjoyment. Be cautious of extravagance and the temptation to overextend yourself during this time. Instead, strive to find balance and moderation in your interactions and pursuits, and avoid making impulsive decisions that could lead to regrets later on.

19 Thursday

The Moon boldly transitions into Aries, igniting the atmosphere with dynamic energy, assertiveness, and a pioneering spirit. During this lunar transition, you may feel a surge of motivation, enthusiasm, and courage to pursue your goals with determination and vigor. Aries' influence encourages you to take initiative, embrace challenges, and assert your individuality with confidence. It's a favorable time for starting new projects, taking risks, and claiming your independence.

20 Friday

At 10:47 AM, celebrate the Vernal March Equinox, marking the beginning of spring in the northern hemisphere and autumn in the southern hemisphere. This astronomical event signifies a moment of balance between day and night as the Sun crosses the celestial equator, bringing equal hours of daylight and darkness. It's a time of renewal, growth, and awakening as nature bursts forth with new life and energy. Embrace the power of the equinox to welcome fresh beginnings.

21 Saturday

Mars forms a harmonious trine aspect with Jupiter, amplifying your energy, enthusiasm, and confidence. This aspect brings a surge of motivation and optimism, inspiring you to pursue your goals with vigor and determination. You may feel a sense of expansion and possibility, as well as a willingness to take risks and explore new opportunities for growth. Use this powerful alignment to channel your energy into endeavors that align with your long-term vision and aspirations.

22 Sunday

At 8:49 PM, you may experience a challenging aspect as Mercury opposes the South Node, indicating a clash between current communication styles, thought patterns, or decisions, and past influences or unresolved issues. This aspect could bring up misunderstandings, delays, or conflicts related to outdated beliefs, communication habits, or information from the past. It's essential to be mindful of any tendencies to revert to old patterns of thinking or communication.

23 Monday

At 4:18 AM, the Moon gracefully transitions into Gemini, infusing the atmosphere with curiosity, versatility, and intellectual stimulation. During this lunar transition, you may feel more inclined to engage in communication, socialize with others, and explore new ideas and perspectives. Gemini's influence encourages you to embrace variety, adaptability, and mental agility as you navigate the world around you. It's a favorable time for learning and networking.

24 Tuesday

Many changes in your life help you improve your bottom line. It offers new possibilities and generates a great deal of forwarding momentum in your life. You shift away from outworn areas and discover the hidden blessings in learning and advancing your talents. Being proactive draws dividends as you climb the ladder to a new level of success in your working life. As you zoom toward new possibilities, you open a prosperous path ahead.

25 Wednesday

The Moon gracefully transitions into Cancer, imbuing the atmosphere with nurturing, emotional sensitivity, and a desire for security and comfort. During this lunar transit, you may feel more attuned to your feelings and those of others, seeking solace in familiar surroundings and meaningful connections with loved ones. Cancer's influence encourages you to prioritize self-care, honor your emotions, and create a supportive environment that nourishes your soul.

26 Thursday

As Venus moves through Aries in your tenth house, you may feel a stronger desire to refine your professional communication and leadership skills. Embrace the opportunity to create a dynamic and supportive approach to your career growth. This period invites you to manifest your goals with clarity and purpose, allowing you to achieve tremendous success and recognition. Engaging in innovative or entrepreneurial projects can enhance your professional reputation.

27 Friday

At 10:10 AM, the Moon gracefully transitions into Leo, infusing the atmosphere with warmth, creativity, and a desire for self-expression. During this lunar transition, you may feel more outgoing, confident, and eager to shine in the spotlight. Leo's influence encourages you to embrace your unique talents, passions, and individuality and to share your light with the world. This period is ideal for engaging in creative endeavors and expressing yourself authentically.

28 Saturday

Saturn forms a harmonious sextile aspect with Pluto, marking a powerful alignment of stability and transformation. This celestial event encourages you to embrace a balanced approach to change and growth, combining discipline and perseverance with a willingness to let go of what no longer serves. Under this influence, you have the determination and resilience to tackle challenges head-on, making constructive changes that have a lasting impact on your life.

29 Sunday

Mercury in Pisces in the ninth house enhances your ability to pursue intellectual and spiritual growth with sensitivity and creativity. You may feel more driven to achieve educational and philosophical goals through intuitive and heartfelt efforts. This is a time to approach your studies and travels with an open heart and a vivid imagination, allowing your sensitivity to new ideas to lead to deeper understanding and meaningful experiences.

APRIL

Mon	Tue	Wed	Thu	Fri	Sat	Sun
		1	2	3	4	5
6	7	8	9	10	11	12
13	14	15	16	17	18	19
20	21	22	23	24	25	26
27	28	29	30			

NEW MOON

PINK MOON

30 Monday

Venus gracefully enters Taurus, infusing the atmosphere with sensuality, beauty, and a deep appreciation for the finer things. During this celestial transition, you may notice a heightened desire for comfort, stability, and indulgence, as Taurus' influence encourages you to savor life's pleasures and surround yourself with luxury. It's a favorable time for cultivating harmony in relationships, indulging in self-care rituals, and enjoying the sensory delights of the physical world.

31 Tuesday

Today, the Libra Moon influence encourages you to seek fairness, compromise, and mutual understanding in your relationships, as well as to appreciate the beauty and harmony in your surroundings. It's a favorable time for cultivating friendships, collaborating on creative projects, and finding equilibrium in your emotions. Embrace the diplomatic energy of the Moon in Libra as you strive to create a sense of balance and beauty in your life and relationships.

1 Wednesday

The Full Moon celestial event illuminates the darkness, inviting you to celebrate achievements, acknowledge progress, and release. Emotions may run high, and insights from the depths of your subconscious may surface, offering valuable messages and revelations. Pay attention to your dreams, intuition, and inner guidance, and embrace the transformative energy of the Full Moon as you surrender to its wisdom and honor the cycles of growth and renewal in your life.

2 Thursday

A new chapter draws beneficial options into your life, giving you a brighter picture of possible possibilities when you stay open to curious leads. Improvement is at the crux of the changes ahead. A lively and productive pathway launches an exciting direction that brings change and opportunity into your world. Something special makes a grand entrance kick off a journey of inspiration and exhilaration. It gets a chance to stimulate creativity and cultivate your talents.

3 Friday

Venus forms a challenging square aspect with Pluto, bringing intensity and power struggles to relationships and financial matters. This aspect may highlight issues of control, manipulation, or obsession, prompting you to confront underlying dynamics and make necessary changes. It's essential to be mindful of power struggles. Use this transit as an opportunity to reassess your values, boundaries, and priorities and to cultivate deeper authenticity.

4 Saturday

Improvement looms overhead as a new influence brings choice opportunities. Cosmic energies reshuffle the decks of potential and offer a unique journey forward. It feeds your spirit with inspiration as you embark on developing new possibilities. Curiosity, guided by celestial forces, is a guiding aspect that points you in the right direction. Life becomes more accessible, expansive, and progressive. You can reach a new level of prosperity driven by universal support.

5 Sunday

The Moon transitions into Sagittarius, infusing the atmosphere with a sense of adventure, optimism, and philosophical exploration. Sagittarius' influence encourages you to embrace new experiences, broaden your horizons, and seek out opportunities for growth and expansion. During this lunar transition, you may feel a strong desire for freedom, spontaneity, and the pursuit of truth. Embrace the adventurous spirit of Sagittarius as you embark on a journey of discovery.

6 Monday

At 5:47 AM, Venus forms both a harmonious sextile aspect with the North Node and a supportive trine aspect with the South Node, creating a celestial alignment that emphasizes the themes of destiny, growth, and karmic connections in relationships and personal development. The sextile to the North Node suggests an opportunity for positive growth and alignment with your soul's path, particularly in matters related to love, creativity, and values.

7 Tuesday

A fresh cycle beckons and helps you move toward new possibilities. Astrological influences give you the green light to cultivate change by working with your creativity and nurturing your talents—clear skies breeze in, bringing curious options to explore. New leads emerge that help you make the most of your abilities as they activate a prosperous chapter of growing security and stability in your life. The universe supports your efforts, making this a time of fruitful exploration.

8 Wednesday

At 12:11 PM, Mars forms a dynamic sextile aspect with Uranus, igniting a spark of innovation, courage, and forward momentum. This alignment empowers you to break free from stagnant routines, embrace change, and take bold, decisive action to pursue your desires. You may feel a surge of energy and confidence, inspiring you to step outside of your comfort zone, experiment with new approaches, and embrace opportunities for growth and liberation.

9 Thursday

At 3:39 PM, Mars, the planet of action and initiative, eagerly enters its home sign of Aries, igniting a surge of fiery energy, courage, and assertiveness. This celestial event marks a decisive shift in the cosmic landscape, as Mars feels right at home in the bold and pioneering sign of Aries. With Mars in Aries, you may feel a renewed sense of vitality, drive, and determination to pursue your goals with passion and enthusiasm.

10 Friday

At 12:52 AM, we reach the Last Quarter Moon, a pivotal phase in the lunar cycle that signifies a time of reflection, release, and preparation for new beginnings. This celestial event prompts you to review your progress, assess what's working and what's not, and let go of anything that no longer serves your highest good. It's an opportunity to release old patterns, beliefs, or situations that are holding you back, clearing the path for fresh opportunities and growth.

11 Saturday

Venus in Taurus in the eleventh house enhances your ability to connect with social networks and community projects with patience and care. You may feel more driven to achieve long-term social and communal objectives through thoughtful and consistent actions. This is a time to approach your social endeavors with a calm and determined mindset. Your ability to communicate your ideas and take the lead in group activities can lead to significant progress and collective success.

12 Sunday

A shift ahead transitions you towards a positive chapter that brings sunny skies overhead. Cosmic energies open the doors to a busy time when you share with friends and family. It brings a positive social aspect that draws well-being and harmony. The universe places you in a solid position to get involved with a more social path, correlating with improved stability on the home front. A social chapter ahead washes away the stress and outworn energy, guided by celestial forces.

APRIL

13 Monday

The Moon in Pisces infuses the atmosphere with sensitivity, compassion, and a dreamy disposition. During this lunar transit, you may find yourself more attuned to your emotions and the subtle energies around you. Pisces' influence encourages you to trust your intuition, engage in creative pursuits, and seek solace in spiritual practices or artistic endeavors. Embrace the gentle, empathetic energy of the Pisces Moon as you navigate your inner world with compassion and grace.

14 Tuesday

Mercury forms a dynamic sextile aspect with Uranus, sparking innovative thinking, original ideas, and intellectual breakthroughs. This celestial alignment encourages you to embrace change, think outside the box, and communicate your ideas with confidence and clarity. Under this influence, you may experience flashes of insight, sudden realizations, or unexpected opportunities for learning and growth. It's a favorable time for brainstorming and problem-solving.

15 Wednesday

At 10:03 AM, the Moon gracefully transitions into Aries, infusing the atmosphere with a surge of dynamic energy, enthusiasm, and initiative. This lunar ingress ignites a fiery and assertive vibe, inspiring you to take action, assert your independence, and pursue your goals with courage and determination. Under the influence of Aries, you may feel a strong desire to initiate new projects, embrace challenges head-on, and assert your individuality with confidence.

16 Thursday

At 2:55 PM, Mars forms a harmonious sextile aspect with Pluto, merging assertiveness with transformative power in a constructive alliance. This celestial alignment imbues you with resilience, determination, and the drive to make significant progress toward your goals. Under this influence, you're empowered to confront challenges with courage and strategic planning, harnessing the intensity of Pluto to effect positive change in your life.

17 Friday

At 11:57 AM, the Moon gracefully transitions into Taurus, grounding the energy and inviting you to cultivate stability, security, and sensual pleasures. In Taurus, you are encouraged to connect with the natural world, indulge in creature comforts, and nurture yourself on a physical level. This lunar transit offers an opportunity to slow down, appreciate the beauty around you, and establish a sense of security and abundance in your life.

18 Saturday

At 4:35 PM, Mercury forms a harmonious sextile aspect with Pluto, creating a powerful alignment of insight, depth, and transformation. Under this celestial influence, you are granted access to profound levels of understanding and the ability to penetrate beneath the surface to uncover hidden truths. This aspect stimulates your mental faculties, empowering you with clarity of thought and the capacity to delve into complex matters with precision and intensity.

19 Sunday

At 12:17 PM, the Moon transitions into Gemini, infusing the atmosphere with curiosity, versatility, and a desire for intellectual stimulation. This lunar ingress encourages you to embrace your curiosity, engage in lively conversations, and explore new ideas and perspectives. Under the influence of Gemini, you may find yourself more friendly, adaptable, and open-minded, eager to connect with others and expand your horizons through communication and learning.

20 Monday

With Mars in Aries transiting your tenth house, your approach to career and public image becomes more assertive and proactive. This period encourages you to take decisive action in pursuing your professional ambitions and achieving recognition. You may find yourself more willing to take on leadership roles and drive forward your career with determination. This is a time to channel your energy into building a successful and impactful professional life.

21 Tuesday

In Cancer, the Moon encourages you to prioritize your emotional well-being, seek comfort in familiar surroundings, and connect with your loved ones on a profound level. You may find yourself more attuned to your feelings and the needs of others, fostering a sense of compassion and empathy. It's a favorable time for introspection, nurturing activities, and creating a safe space where you can express your emotions authentically.

22 Wednesday

With Mercury in Aries transiting your tenth house, your approach to career and public image becomes more dynamic and assertive. This period encourages you to focus on achieving professional success through confident and proactive efforts. You may find yourself more willing to take the lead in tasks that require a bold approach. This is a time to channel your mental energy into building a stable and prosperous professional life.

23 Thursday

In Leo, the Moon encourages you to embrace your individuality, shine brightly, and express yourself with confidence and flair. You may feel a surge of creativity and passion, inspiring you to pursue your creative endeavors and share your unique talents. It's a favorable time for embracing your inner artist, stepping into the spotlight, and basking in the joy of self-expression. Embrace the radiant energy of the Leo Moon as you honor your creativity and celebrate your uniqueness.

24 Friday

At 12:05 AM, Venus gracefully transitions into Gemini, infusing the atmosphere with curiosity, sociability, and a desire for variety in relationships and pleasures. In Gemini, Venus encourages you to embrace diversity, engage in stimulating conversations, and explore different facets of love and connection. You may find yourself more inclined to seek out intellectual connections, flirtation, and playful interactions with others.

25 Saturday

At 9:35 PM, Uranus enters Gemini, initiating a period of intellectual awakening, innovation, and unpredictability. In Gemini, Uranus prompts you to embrace change with an open mind, explore new ideas and perspectives, and adapt to unexpected shifts in your environment. This transit may bring about exciting breakthroughs in communication, technology, and social interactions, encouraging you to embrace your individuality and express yourself freely.

26 Sunday

Mercury squares Jupiter, creating a dynamic interplay between intellect, expansion, and exaggeration. This aspect warns against overconfidence, excessive optimism, or overlooking important details in communication or decision-making. You may feel inclined to take on too much without considering the practicalities involved. It's essential to temper your enthusiasm with a healthy dose of realism and maintain a balanced perspective to avoid over-commitment.

27 Monday

The Sun trine South Node suggests a harmonious integration of past experiences and wisdom into your present life. It indicates that you can draw upon insights gained from your history with ease and confidence. You may find yourself naturally embodying the strengths and lessons learned from previous chapters, guiding you toward greater self-awareness and fulfillment. It's a time for acknowledging and honoring the valuable contributions of your past.

28 Tuesday

In Libra, the Moon encourages you to seek harmony and cooperation in your interactions, prioritize fairness and justice, and cultivate a sense of peace and beauty in your environment. You may find yourself drawn to activities that promote socializing, diplomacy, and artistic expression, making it an ideal time for fostering connections, resolving conflicts, and appreciating the aesthetics of life. Strive for equilibrium and cultivate connections based on mutual respect.

29 Wednesday

The square with the South Node suggests that you may be confronted with unresolved issues, patterns, or attachments from the past that hinder your ability to experience fulfillment and harmony in your relationships. This aspect encourages you to release old patterns, let go of limiting beliefs, and break free from unhealthy relationship dynamics that no longer serve your growth and evolution. It's a time for soul-searching, healing, and reclaiming your power.

30 Thursday

In Scorpio, the Moon encourages you to delve into the depths of your psyche, uncover hidden truths, and embrace transformation. You may find yourself drawn to introspection, seeking to understand the deeper motivations behind your emotions and behaviors. This lunar transit heightens your intuition and sensitivity, allowing you to penetrate beneath the surface and explore the complexities of human nature.

MAY

Mon	Tue	Wed	Thu	Fri	Sat	Sun
				1	2	3
4	5	6	7	8	9	10
11	12	13	14	15	16	17
18	19	20	21	22	23	24
25	26	27	28	29	30	31

NEW MOON

_____

_____

_____

_____

_____

_____

_____

_____

_____

_____

_____

_____

_____

_____

_____

_____

_____

_____

_____

_____

FLOWER MOON

MAY

1 Friday

Venus forms a harmonious sextile aspect with Saturn, creating a supportive alignment of love, commitment, and stability. This celestial combination infuses your relationships with a sense of responsibility, maturity, and long-term planning. You may find yourself more inclined to honor your commitments, strengthen bonds with loved ones, and build a solid foundation for lasting connections. It's a favorable time for investing in relationships.

2 Saturday

In Taurus, Mercury encourages practical thinking, grounded communication, and a deliberate approach to decision-making. You may find yourself drawn to tangible, sensory experiences and inclined towards patience and perseverance in your thoughts and conversations. This transit fosters a deeper appreciation for stability, security, and material well-being, prompting you to prioritize practicality and reliability in your interactions and mental processes.

3 Sunday

The Moon gracefully transitions into Sagittarius, infusing the atmosphere with adventurous, optimistic, and expansive energy. In Sagittarius, the Moon encourages you to embrace freedom, seek new experiences, and broaden your horizons. You may feel a strong urge to explore unfamiliar territories, both physically and mentally, as you seek out new perspectives and opportunities for growth. This lunar transit ignites a sense of wanderlust and a desire for adventure.

4 Monday

Mars forms a challenging square aspect with Jupiter, marking a time of heightened energy, ambition, and potential conflicts. This celestial alignment can bring a surge of enthusiasm and drive, motivating you to pursue your goals with zeal and determination. However, there is a risk of overestimating your abilities or taking on too much at once, leading to impulsive actions or conflicts with authority figures. It's essential to channel this powerful energy in productive ways.

5 Tuesday

At 3:06 PM, the Moon transitions into Capricorn, marking a shift towards a more disciplined, pragmatic, and goal-oriented emotional energy. In Capricorn, the Moon encourages you to prioritize responsibilities, set ambitious goals, and approach tasks with a sense of determination and purpose. You may find yourself more focused on long-term plans, career matters, and practical concerns during this lunar transition.

6 Wednesday

The square with the South Node highlights potential challenges or obstacles related to past patterns, beliefs, or communication habits that may hinder your progress. You may find yourself confronted with old thought patterns, limiting beliefs, or unresolved issues from the past that require your attention and transformation. It's essential to recognize any unconscious patterns or tendencies that no longer serve your highest good and consciously choose to release them.

7 Thursday

With the Sun in Taurus transiting your ninth house, your focus on higher learning, travel, and spiritual growth becomes more patient and practical. This period encourages you to seek out new experiences that expand your horizons and challenge your beliefs. You may feel more motivated to pursue educational opportunities, embark on journeys, and explore new philosophies. It is a time to channel your energy into broadening your understanding of the world.

8 Friday

In Aquarius, the Moon encourages you to embrace your individuality, think outside the box, and pursue unconventional solutions to challenges. You may feel drawn to social causes, group activities, and intellectual pursuits that promote progress and social change. This lunar transit inspires you to connect with like-minded individuals, share ideas, and collaborate on projects that have the potential to benefit the collective.

9 Saturday

The Last Quarter phase encourages you to take stock of your experiences and achievements since the beginning of the lunar cycle, identify what is no longer serving your highest good, and gracefully release any burdens, habits, or emotions that are holding you back. It's a potent moment for surrendering to the natural rhythms of endings and beginnings, trusting in the wisdom of the lunar cycle to guide you on your journey of personal evolution and renewal.

10 Sunday

The Sun forms a harmonious sextile aspect with Jupiter, creating an expansive and optimistic atmosphere that inspires growth, abundance, and opportunities for expansion. This celestial alignment encourages you to embrace a positive outlook, take bold leaps of faith, and pursue your goals with confidence and enthusiasm. You may feel a sense of optimism and possibility permeating your endeavors, fueling your aspirations and opening doors to new opportunities.

11 Monday

With Mercury in Taurus transiting your eleventh house, your approach to social networks and community involvement becomes more practical and reliable. This period encourages you to build meaningful connections and actively pursue your aspirations with a steady and thoughtful mindset. You may find yourself engaging in group activities that benefit from a practical approach. It is a time to channel your mental energy into creating a supportive and enduring social network.

12 Tuesday

At 8:03 PM, the Moon shifts into Aries, infusing the atmosphere with a dynamic and assertive energy. In Aries, the Moon encourages you to embrace courage, initiative, and a pioneering spirit. You may feel a surge of motivation and enthusiasm, propelling you to take decisive action and pursue your goals with passion. This lunar transit ignites your inner fire and inspires you to assert your independence, assert your needs, and boldly venture into new territory.

13 Wednesday

Mercury forms a harmonious sextile aspect with Jupiter, creating a synergistic blend of intellect and expansive energy. This celestial alignment enhances your mental faculties, facilitating clear communication, optimistic thinking, and broad-mindedness. You may find yourself more open to new ideas, eager to learn, and inclined to engage in philosophical or intellectual discussions. Under this influence, your thoughts may be infused with enthusiasm and optimism.

14 Thursday

At 10:31 PM, the Moon gracefully transitions into Taurus, ushering in a period characterized by stability, comfort, and sensual pleasures. In Taurus, the Moon encourages you to slow down, indulge in creature comforts, and cultivate a sense of security and tranquility in your surroundings. You may find yourself drawn to activities that engage your senses, such as enjoying good food, surrounding yourself with beauty, or spending time in nature.

15 Friday

With Venus in Gemini transiting your twelfth house, your approach to introspection, spirituality, and hidden matters becomes more dynamic and communicative. You may find yourself focusing on practical ways to understand your subconscious mind and explore spiritual practices through intellectual and social interaction. This period encourages you to embrace a lively and versatile approach to self-discovery and inner growth.

16 Saturday

The New Moon heralds the beginning of a lunar cycle, symbolizing new beginnings and opportunities for growth. This celestial event occurs when the Moon aligns with the Sun, marking a potent moment for setting intentions, planting seeds of intention, and initiating projects that align with your long-term goals. The New Moon encourages a spirit of optimism, innovation, and possibility as you embark on a journey of self-discovery and manifestation.

17 Sunday

In its home sign of Gemini, Mercury amplifies curiosity, adaptability, and versatility, encouraging you to embrace intellectual exploration and engage in lively exchanges with others. This celestial alignment enhances your ability to express yourself with wit, charm, and eloquence, making it an ideal time for networking, brainstorming, and gathering information from various sources. You may find yourself more open to new ideas and eager to learn.

MAY

18 Monday

At 9:46 PM, the Moon enters Cancer, amplifying the nurturing and intuitive energies of this sign. In its and your sign of Cancer, the Moon heightens emotional sensitivity and fosters a deep connection to your innermost feelings and desires. You may find yourself more attuned to the needs of your loved ones and more inclined to seek solace and security within the comforts of home. This lunar transit encourages you to listen to your intuition and honor your emotions.

19 Tuesday

At 6:52 PM, Mercury forms a harmonious trine aspect with Pluto, empowering your mental clarity, insight, and ability to penetrate beneath the surface to uncover hidden truths. This aspect enhances your ability to dive deep into complex issues, research, or psychological analysis with precision and depth. You may find yourself drawn to investigative work, problem-solving, or uncovering secrets that have been buried beneath the surface.

20 Wednesday

Together, the Sun in Gemini and the Moon in Leo create a dynamic blend of intellectual curiosity and creative self-expression. It's a time to explore new ideas, engage in stimulating conversations, and infuse your interactions with warmth, generosity, and enthusiasm. Embrace the playful and vibrant energy of this combination as you seek to express yourself authentically, connect with others on a deeper level, and embrace the joy of living life to the fullest.

21 Thursday

Saturn in Aries in the tenth house enhances your ability to pursue career goals with a sense of seriousness and commitment. You may feel more focused on building a solid and reputable professional identity. This is a time to approach your career with a structured and systematic mindset. Your ability to set clear goals and work diligently towards them can lead to significant achievements and professional growth.

22 Friday

Venus trines both the North Node and the South Node, aligning the energies of love, karma, and destiny in a harmonious and supportive manner. These aspects may bring significant opportunities for growth, evolution, and karmic connections in your relationships. You may feel a sense of alignment with your soul's journey and a deep resonance with your heart's desires. It's a favorable time for forming meaningful connections and reconciling past issues.

23 Saturday

At 7:12 AM, the Moon reaches its First Quarter phase, marking a pivotal moment in the lunar cycle. This phase encourages you to take action, make decisions, and overcome any obstacles that stand in the way of your goals. It's a time for setting intentions, assessing your progress, and adjusting your course as needed. The First Quarter Moon prompts you to step out of your comfort zone, embrace challenges, and move forward with confidence and determination.

24 Sunday

At 9:56 PM, Mars simultaneously forms sextile and trine aspects with the North Node and the South Node, highlighting themes of destiny, action, and karmic growth. These aspects may bring about opportunities for assertive action, personal development, and alignment with your soul's purpose. You may feel a sense of motivation, drive, and determination to pursue your goals and aspirations, as well as a willingness to take bold risks and step outside your comfort zone.

25 Monday

At 10:34 AM, the Moon gracefully transitions into Libra, ushering in a period characterized by harmony, balance, and a focus on relationships. In Libra, the lunar energy becomes diplomatic, pleasant, and oriented towards seeking peace and harmony in interactions with others. This lunar transit encourages you to cultivate fairness, cooperation, and diplomacy in your relationships, as well as to find the balance between your own needs and the needs of others.

26 Tuesday

At 12:01 AM, Mars forms a challenging square aspect with Pluto, igniting intense and transformative energies that may bring power struggles, conflicts, or confrontations to the forefront. This aspect can stir up deep-seated emotions, desires, and drives, leading to feelings of frustration, anger, or compulsion. It's crucial to channel this potent energy constructively and avoid getting drawn into power struggles or coercive tactics.

27 Wednesday

As the Moon journeys through Scorpio, you may find yourself drawn to activities that involve deep introspection, research, or investigation. It's an excellent time for therapy, journaling, or any form of psychological exploration that allows you to delve into the depths of your soul. You may also feel a heightened desire for intimacy and emotional connection, seeking to forge deep and meaningful bonds with others based on trust, honesty, and authenticity.

28 Thursday

Venus forms a challenging square aspect with Saturn, creating a tense and restrictive energy in matters of love, relationships, and finances. This aspect may bring about feelings of limitation, duty, and responsibility in your interactions with others, as well as obstacles or delays in romantic or creative endeavors. You may experience a sense of distance or coldness in your relationships, as well as a need to confront any underlying issues that are lingering beneath the surface.

29 Friday

Venus in Cancer in the First House enhances your ability to initiate new relationships and create a nurturing foundation for self-growth. You may feel more driven to assert your needs and desires in a caring and empathetic manner, making it easier to pursue your personal goals with sensitivity and compassion. This is a time to explore new ways of presenting yourself and to embrace the beauty of emotional depth and intuition in your self-expression.

30 Saturday

In Sagittarius, the lunar energy becomes enthusiastic, freedom-loving, and philosophical, encouraging you to embrace new experiences, explore different perspectives, and expand your horizons. This lunar transit may inspire you to seek out knowledge, travel to unfamiliar places, or engage in activities that broaden your understanding of the world and your place within it. You may feel a renewed sense of optimism, as well as a desire to embrace life with a spirit of adventure.

31 Sunday

Under the influence of the Sagittarius Full Moon, you are urged to embrace a sense of adventure, expansion, and freedom. Sagittarius encourages you to explore new horizons, expand your mind, and pursue your beliefs and ideals with passion and enthusiasm. You may feel a strong urge to break free from limitations, embrace spontaneity, and seek out new experiences that nourish your soul and ignite your sense of purpose.

JUNE

Mon	Tue	Wed	Thu	Fri	Sat	Sun
1	2	3	4	5	6	7
8	9	10	11	12	13	14
15	16	17	18	19	20	21
22	23	24	25	26	27	28
29	30					

NEW MOON

STRAWBERRY MOON

JUNE

1 Monday

In Capricorn, the lunar energy becomes disciplined, goal-oriented, and focused on long-term success. This lunar transit encourages you to take a grounded and pragmatic approach to your emotions, responsibilities, and goals. You may feel motivated to set clear intentions, work diligently towards your objectives, and take on leadership roles with confidence and determination. Use this time to establish solid foundations, organize your priorities, and pursue your ambitions.

2 Tuesday

At 6:48 PM, the Sun forms a harmonious sextile aspect with Saturn, blending the energies of vitality and structure in a supportive and constructive manner. This celestial alignment brings a sense of stability, discipline, and practicality to your endeavors, empowering you to make steady progress toward your long-term goals. You may find yourself feeling more grounded, responsible, and focused as you work diligently to lay solid foundations for future success.

3 Wednesday

At 7:39 AM, Mercury forms both a harmonious trine aspect with the North Node and a supportive sextile aspect with the South Node, marking a significant moment for communication, learning, and karmic evolution. These aspects suggest opportunities for aligning your thoughts and communication with your soul's purpose. You may find yourself drawn to meaningful conversations, insightful insights, and synchronicities that guide you along your path.

4 Thursday

At 9:45 AM, the Moon transitions into Aquarius, infusing the atmosphere with an air of innovation, individuality, and humanitarianism. In Aquarius, the lunar energy becomes progressive, unconventional, and forward-thinking, inspiring you to embrace your uniqueness, express your authentic self, and contribute to the collective in meaningful ways. This lunar transit encourages you to break from societal norms, explore new ideas, and connect with like-minded individuals.

5 Friday

Mars in Taurus in the eleventh house enhances your ability to build solid and reliable friendships and engage in community activities with determination and patience. You may feel more driven to achieve social and community goals through consistent and practical efforts. It is a time to approach your social interactions with a grounded and steady mindset, allowing your persistence to foster deeper connections.

6 Saturday

With Pisces Moon, your intuitive faculties are heightened, inviting you to trust your inner guidance and explore the realms of dreams and fantasies. Your imagination knows no bounds, and you may draw mystical or spiritual pursuits that offer insight into the mysteries of life. It's a time to embrace compassion, forgiveness, and unconditional love, both for yourself and for those around you. Allow yourself to find beauty and meaning in the subtle nuances of existence.

7 Sunday

With Mercury in Cancer transiting your first house, your communication style becomes more intuitive and nurturing. This period encourages you to express yourself with a focus on emotional depth and sensitivity. You may find yourself more inclined to share your feelings and personal insights. This is a time to channel your mental energy into individual projects that benefit from empathetic and heartfelt communication.

8 Monday

As the Moon enters its Last Quarter phase at 6:01 AM, you're encouraged to embrace the opportunity for introspection and reassessment. This phase invites you to take stock of your journey, acknowledging both your successes and setbacks with honesty and clarity. By confronting any lingering doubts or uncertainties head-on, you can gain valuable insights into your path forward. Trust in your inner wisdom and intuition as you navigate this period of transition.

9 Tuesday

With the Moon's ingress into Aries at 4:33 AM, you may feel a surge of energy and assertiveness propelling you towards action. This lunar transit ignites a fiery passion within you, inspiring courage, initiative, and a desire to take charge of your life. You're driven by a sense of independence and individuality, eager to pursue your goals with enthusiasm and determination. Embrace this invigorating energy to initiate new beginnings and tackle challenges head-on.

10 Wednesday

When Mercury squares Saturn at 1:37 AM, you might encounter challenges in communication and mental tasks due to Saturn's restrictive influence. This aspect could bring about feelings of frustration, delays, or obstacles in expressing yourself effectively. Your thoughts may feel burdened by responsibilities or limitations, leading to a cautious approach to problem-solving. This transit encourages you to confront and overcome obstacles through disciplined focus and practical thinking.

11 Thursday

Today is a favorable time for indulging in self-care activities, nurturing yourself and loved ones, and creating a harmonious environment. It's also a time when financial matters and material security may come into focus, prompting you to seek stability and security in these areas. Overall, the Moon's ingress into Taurus encourages you to slow down, enjoy the present moment, and cultivate a sense of peace and contentment in your life.

12 Friday

At 2:43 PM, Uranus forms a square aspect both with the North Node and the South Node, indicating a period of dynamic change and potential upheaval in your karmic path. This aspect challenges you to break free from past patterns and embrace new ways of being that align with your future growth and evolution. You may feel a strong urge to liberate yourself from limitations and restrictions, but be mindful of impulsive actions or rebellion for its own sake.

13 Saturday

Venus gracefully transitions into Leo, infusing your relationships, values, and aesthetic preferences with the vibrant energy of the lion-hearted sign. This ingress brings a sense of warmth, creativity, and passion to your interactions and desires. You may find yourself craving attention, recognition, and romance, and your expressions of love become bold, dramatic, and generous. Under this influence, you're encouraged to embrace your uniqueness and express yourself authentically.

14 Sunday

The New Moon, which occurs at 10:55 PM, heralds a potent moment for new beginnings and setting intentions. New Moons represent a time of initiation and planting seeds for the future, making it an optimal moment for setting goals, starting projects, or initiating changes in your life. This lunar phase encourages introspection, reflection, and envisioning the path ahead. With the darkness of the Moon, there is a sense of fertile potentiality, offering opportunities for growth.

15 Monday

The Moon moves into your sign of Cancer, marking a shift in emotional focus towards nurturing, security, and sensitivity. This ingress encourages a desire for comfort, home, and familiar surroundings. You may find yourself more attuned to your emotions and those of others, seeking emotional connections and a sense of belonging. It's a time to prioritize self-care, spend time with loved ones, and create a supportive environment that nurtures your emotional well-being.

16 Tuesday

At 11:40 PM, Venus forms a harmonious trine with Neptune, inviting you to embrace a heightened sense of romance, creativity, and spiritual connection. This aspect infuses your relationships and aesthetic sensibilities with a dreamy and compassionate energy, fostering a deep sense of empathy and understanding in your interactions with others. You may find yourself drawn to expressions of beauty, art, and music that evoke a sense of magic and enchantment.

17 Wednesday

Navigating today's Venus-Pluto opposition requires honesty, transparency, and a willingness to delve into the depths of your emotions. It's crucial to approach relationship dynamics with integrity, communicate openly, and avoid power struggles or manipulative behaviors. This cosmic alignment catalyzes growth, inviting you to release old patterns, heal emotional wounds, and embrace authentic connections based on mutual respect and understanding.

18 Thursday

A celestial influence encourages you to embrace change with an open heart and mind, guiding you toward new horizons where innovative ideas and fresh perspectives will fuel your creativity and propel you toward tremendous success and personal satisfaction. This time of change will also bring unexpected opportunities that challenge you to grow and adapt, ultimately making you more resilient and versatile in the face of life's challenges.

19 Friday

At 10:37 AM, the Moon transitions into meticulous Virgo, marking a shift in the cosmic energies towards practicality, organization, and attention to detail. During this lunar ingress, you may feel a stronger urge to focus on productivity, efficiency, and improving various aspects of your daily life. Virgo's influence encourages you to analyze, plan, and strive for perfection in your work, health routines, and daily tasks. It is an excellent time to prioritize your well-being.

20 Saturday

With Venus in Leo transiting your second house, your approach to finances and material possessions becomes more confident and extravagant. You may find yourself focusing on practical ways to enhance your financial security and attract new sources of income through charismatic and creative interactions. This period encourages you to embrace a bold and expressive approach to wealth, blending your determination with a desire for luxury and recognition.

21 Sunday

At 4:27 AM, the Sun enters your sign of Cancer, initiating a new astrological season characterized by nurturing, emotional sensitivity, and a focus on home and family. Cancer's influence encourages you to prioritize your emotional well-being, connect with loved ones, and create a secure and nurturing environment. It is a time for introspection, deepening emotional bonds, and seeking comfort and stability in your personal life.

22 Monday

The cosmos is sending waves of transformative energy your way, enabling you to break free from past limitations and embark on a journey of self-discovery and growth that will unlock new potentials and enrich your life with unparalleled experiences and achievements. This period of transformation will empower you to redefine your goals and pursue them with renewed vigor, leading to a profound sense of fulfillment and purpose.

23 Tuesday

The Sun sextiles the South Node while reinforcing this theme of karmic evolution and alignment. The sextile aspect represents a supportive and harmonious energy flow between the Sun and the point where the Moon's path crosses the ecliptic from north to south. This aspect encourages you to integrate lessons from the past, release old patterns or limitations, and embrace new possibilities for growth and transformation.

24 Wednesday

Under the influence of the Moon in Scorpio, you may experience heightened sensitivity, intuition, and a desire to delve beneath the surface of things. This astrological placement encourages you to confront hidden truths, address emotional complexities, and embrace the process of regeneration and rebirth. It's a period conducive to psychological healing, releasing emotional baggage, and gaining insights into your subconscious motivations.

25 Thursday

When Venus forms a trine with Saturn at 8:01 AM, it sets a tone of stability, commitment, and practicality in matters of love, relationships, and creativity. This harmonious aspect between Venus and Saturn brings a sense of responsibility and maturity to your interactions and endeavors. You may find that your romantic relationships or creative projects benefit from a structured approach, long-term planning, and a focus on building solid foundations.

26 Friday

The Sagittarius Moon fosters a positive outlook and encourages you to focus on the bigger picture rather than getting bogged down by minor details or restrictions. It's a time for optimism, forward-thinking, and embracing opportunities that align with your long-term goals and aspirations. Use this lunar transit to tap into your sense of adventure, embrace new possibilities, and pursue personal growth with a sense of enthusiasm and openness.

27 Saturday

With the Sun in Cancer transiting your first house, your focus is on personal identity, self-expression, and emotional well-being. This period encourages you to connect with your inner self and nurture your emotional needs. You may feel more inclined to express your feelings openly and create a sense of security in your personal life. Use this time to prioritize self-care and develop a deeper understanding of your emotional landscape.

28 Sunday

The Mars-Jupiter sextile inspires you to think big, take calculated risks, and push past limitations to achieve your ambitions. It encourages a positive mindset, resilience in the face of challenges, and a belief in your abilities to overcome obstacles and reach new heights. It is an excellent time for initiating projects, asserting yourself assertively but diplomatically, and tapping into your inner strength and determination.

JULY

Mon	Tue	Wed	Thu	Fri	Sat	Sun
		1	2	3	4	5
6	7	8	9	10	11	12
13	14	15	16	17	18	19
20	21	22	23	24	25	26
27	28	29	30	31		

NEW MOON

_____

_____

_____

_____

_____

_____

_____

_____

_____

_____

_____

_____

_____

_____

_____

_____

_____

_____

_____

_____

BUCK MOON

30 Monday

Mercury turns retrograde, initiating a period of introspection, review, and potential communication challenges. During Mercury retrograde, it's advisable to double-check details and avoid signing contracts or making significant decisions without thorough consideration. This phase invites you to revisit past ideas, projects, and connections, offering an opportunity to resolve misunderstandings, clarify intentions, and reassess your strategies moving forward.

31 Tuesday

A significant planetary shift occurs at 2:07 AM, with Jupiter ingressing into Leo. This ingress brings a surge of confidence, creativity, and enthusiasm. Jupiter in Leo encourages you to embrace your individuality, express yourself boldly, and pursue your passions with optimism and joy. This transit favors self-expression, creativity, and expanding your horizons through artistic endeavors, leadership roles, or taking risks with a sense of adventure.

1 Wednesday

The Aquarius Moon encourages you to trust your intuition, embrace your eccentricities, and express your authentic self without fear of judgment. It's a time to celebrate individuality, embrace diversity, and contribute your unique perspective to the world around you. Embrace the innovative and progressive energy of the Aquarius Moon to spark creativity, inspire positive change, and cultivate a sense of unity within your community and beyond.

2 Thursday

The Sun in Cancer in the First House enhances your ability to connect with others on an emotional level. You're likely to be more empathetic and caring, making this an excellent time to strengthen your relationships. This influence can bring about a period of personal growth as you explore your emotional needs and express yourself authentically. By staying true to your feelings and nurturing your well-being, you can create a harmonious and fulfilling life.

JULY
3 Friday

With Mars in Gemini transiting your twelfth house, your approach to introspection and spirituality becomes more dynamic and curious. This period encourages you to explore your inner world and address subconscious issues with enthusiasm and adaptability. You may find yourself more willing to engage in spiritual practices and work through hidden challenges innovatively. This is a time to channel your energy into creating inner strength and self-discovery.

4 Saturday

Mars forms a sextile aspect with Neptune, adding a dose of inspiration, creativity, and spiritual alignment to the atmosphere. This harmonious alignment between the action-oriented Mars and the mystical Neptune brings opportunities for creative expression, intuitive insights, and tapping into your inner vision. It's a favorable time for pursuing artistic endeavors, spiritual practices, or activities that allow you to channel your energy into meaningful and soul-nourishing pursuits.

5 Sunday

When Mars forms a trine aspect with Pluto at 9:06 AM, a potent and transformative energy permeates the day. This harmonious alignment between the assertive Mars and the powerful Pluto brings a surge of determination, resilience, and intensity to your actions and endeavors. You may feel a strong sense of purpose, drive, and motivation to overcome challenges, make significant changes, and pursue your ambitions with confidence and strength.

6 Monday

Overall, today's astrological influences of the Sun square Saturn and the Moon ingressing Aries present a dynamic blend of challenges and opportunities for personal growth. Embrace the lessons of discipline and responsibility from the Sun-Saturn aspect while harnessing the bold, assertive energy of the Aries Moon to take decisive action, pursue your ambitions, and navigate obstacles with determination and resilience.

7 Tuesday

At 7:40 AM, Neptune begins its retrograde motion, marking a period of introspection, spiritual reflection, and internal exploration. When Neptune turns retrograde, it encourages you to delve deep into your subconscious, dreams, and spiritual beliefs. This cosmic shift invites you to review illusions, fantasies, and idealizations, gaining clarity and insight into areas where illusions may have clouded your perception. Use this time to reconnect with your inner wisdom.

8 Wednesday

Today is a time to slow down, savor moments of relaxation, and cultivate gratitude for the abundance and beauty that surrounds you. Use this period to ground yourself, align with your values, and create a sense of security and stability in both your inner and outer worlds. Embrace the nurturing energy of the Taurus Moon as you create a harmonious and supportive environment that reflects your values and brings you joy.

9 Thursday

Under the influence of Venus in Virgo, you may feel a desire to improve your daily routines, create a nurturing environment, and pay attention to the small gestures that enhance well-being and connection. It is a favorable time for tending to practical matters in relationships, such as planning, organizing, and showing appreciation through thoughtful actions. Embrace this period to cultivate a sense of order, efficiency, and mindfulness in matters of the heart.

10 Friday

Overall, today's astrological influences highlight the themes of balance in relationships and intellectual curiosity. Embrace the challenges and growth opportunities presented by the Venus opposition North Node aspect while also enjoying the lively and communicative energy of the Gemini Moon's ingress. Use this time to foster meaningful connections, engage in stimulating conversations, and align your actions with your evolving understanding of love and harmony.

11 Saturday

As you move through the day, remain vigilant yet open-hearted, embracing each moment with a spirit of curiosity and humility. Recognize that within the subtle whispers of the universe lie hidden treasures of insight and revelation, guiding you toward greater understanding and enlightenment. Allow yourself to be guided by the currents of cosmic energy, finding solace and guidance in the sanctuary of your inner knowing as you journey through the celestial symphony of life.

12 Sunday

Under the influence of the Cancer Moon, you may feel more attuned to your emotions, seeking solace in familiar surroundings and finding fulfillment in caring for yourself and others. It is a favorable time for introspection, self-care practices, and creating a supportive and nurturing environment that nourishes your soul. Embrace this period to connect with your innermost feelings, express your emotions authentically, and cultivate a sense of inner peace and harmony.

13 Monday

Use this time to embrace change, embrace your unique qualities, and cultivate flexibility and adaptability in your approach to relationships and personal values. Allow yourself to explore new horizons, embrace diversity, and find creative solutions to any challenges that arise during the dynamic aspect between Venus and Uranus. Trust in your ability to navigate unexpected situations with grace and authenticity, finding opportunities for growth and liberation along the way.

14 Tuesday

Today's astrological influences highlight a blend of new beginnings and expressive energies. Harness the power of the New Moon to set intentions and lay the foundation for future growth and success. As the Moon enters Leo, embrace your creativity, confidence, and desire for self-expression, allowing your unique light to shine brightly in all that you do. Embrace the possibilities of new beginnings and express yourself boldly, knowing that the universe supports your growth.

15 Wednesday

The Uranus-Neptune sextile invites you to explore spiritual and metaphysical realms, seeking a more profound understanding and connection to universal truths. This aspect supports practices such as meditation, visualization, and creative expression as pathways to accessing higher wisdom and inner guidance. Embrace this opportunity to delve into your spiritual journey, connect with your inner wisdom, and cultivate a sense of peace and harmony within.

16 Thursday

Under the influence of the Virgo Moon, you may feel more inclined to pay attention to the details, prioritize tasks, and strive for perfection in your daily routines. This lunar ingress fosters a sense of productivity, practicality, and a desire to improve and refine your environment and habits. Take this time to break down larger tasks into manageable steps, set realistic goals, and create a schedule that allows you to be efficient while maintaining balance in your life.

17 Friday

Venus in Virgo in the third house enhances your ability to communicate with precision and thoughtfulness. You may feel more driven to achieve intellectual goals through meticulous and analytical efforts. This is a time to approach your studies and communication with a careful and organized mindset. Your ability to articulate your ideas and engage in meaningful discussions can lead to significant progress and deeper connections.

18 Saturday

The harmonious aspect between Uranus and Pluto encourages you to explore innovative ideas, pursue creative endeavors, and make bold changes that align with your vision for the future. It's a favorable time for exploring new technologies, unconventional solutions, and progressive approaches to problem-solving. Embrace your inner revolutionary spirit and embrace opportunities to make a positive impact in your life and the world around you.

19 Sunday

The Mars-Saturn sextile aspect empowers you to progress, overcome obstacles, and achieve long-term success through focused effort and disciplined action. It's a favorable time for planning, organization, and implementing strategies that lead to tangible results. Embrace this aspect to cultivate resilience, strengthen your commitments, and take responsible action towards your aspirations. Trust your abilities, stay disciplined, and remain focused on your goals.

20 Monday

When Jupiter forms a trine aspect with Neptune, a harmonious and spiritually uplifting energy permeates the cosmic realm, bringing a sense of inspiration, intuition, and idealism. This aspect combines the expansive and optimistic nature of Jupiter with the dreamy and imaginative qualities of Neptune, creating a fertile ground for creativity, spiritual growth, and inner exploration. Embrace this celestial alignment as an invitation to expand your horizons.

21 Tuesday

today's astrological influences highlight a blend of action, innovation, and emotional depth. Embrace the momentum of the First Quarter Moon to propel your plans forward, harness the Jupiter-Uranus sextile's energy to embrace change and creativity, and navigate the Scorpio Moon's intensity with courage, authenticity, and a willingness to explore the depths of your emotions and experiences. Embrace the opportunities for growth and expansion.

22 Wednesday

When the Sun enters Leo at 3:16 PM, a vibrant and radiant energy fills the cosmos, ushering in a period of creativity, self-expression, and confidence. This astrological event marks the beginning of Leo season, highlighting themes of passion, leadership, and embracing one's unique identity. As the Sun transitions into Leo, you're encouraged to tap into your inner fire, express yourself, and shine your light brightly. This solar ingress ignites a sense of vitality and enthusiasm.

23 Thursday

When Mercury turns direct at 6:58 PM, a shift in communication and mental clarity occurs, allowing for smoother conversations, clearer thinking, and progress in plans and projects that may have been delayed or stalled during its retrograde period. This astrological event brings a sense of relief and forward momentum, making it an ideal time to resolve misunderstandings, finalize agreements, and move forward with confidence in decision-making.

24 Friday

Overall, the Mercury-Venus sextile invites you to embrace harmonious communication, express your feelings authentically, and appreciate the beauty and creativity around you. Use this time to nurture your relationships, express love and gratitude, and engage in activities that uplift your spirit and inspire creativity. Trust in the power of heartfelt communication and let your words and actions reflect your genuine feelings and intentions.

25 Saturday

The Neptune-Pluto sextile offers a profound opportunity for spiritual growth, inner healing, and transformation. Deepen your connection with the divine, release wounds, and step into authentic power with grace and wisdom. Trust in the process of inner alchemy and allow yourself to be guided by the higher forces of the universe as you navigate your spiritual evolution. Open your heart to the wisdom of the cosmos and allow the energies of Neptune and Pluto to guide you.

26 Sunday

Overall, today's astrological influences encourage you to embrace responsibility, discipline, and alignment with your higher purpose. Use the Capricorn Moon's influence to focus on productivity and long-term planning, navigate Saturn's retrograde with introspection and self-improvement, and embrace the nodal shifts towards collective progress and personal growth. Trust in the process of evolution and make conscious choices that align with your values and aspirations.

27 Monday

Overall, today's astrological influences offer a mix of intensity, inspiration, and innovation. Navigate the Sun's opposition to Pluto with awareness and empowerment, harness the Sun's trine with Neptune to nurture your spiritual and creative side, and embrace the Sun's sextile with Uranus to embrace change and explore new horizons. Trust in your inner strength, follow your intuition, and embrace the transformative energies guiding you toward growth and evolution.

28 Tuesday

The Aquarius Moon encourages you to cultivate emotional detachment and objectivity, allowing you to approach situations with a clear mind and a focus on rationality. Embrace your ability to see the bigger picture, seek unconventional solutions, and contribute your unique perspective to collective endeavors. Use your intellectual curiosity and open-mindedness to navigate complexities with clarity and innovation, fostering a sense of unity and progress.

29 Wednesday

Today's astrological influences highlight the importance of finding harmony in relationships, embracing emotional awareness, and aligning your actions with your intentions. Navigate conflicts with compassion and communication, and use the Full Moon's illuminating energy to gain insights, release emotional baggage, and move towards greater fulfillment and authenticity in your life. Trust in the transformative power of self-awareness and conscious choices.

30 Thursday

With the Sun in Leo transiting your second house, your focus is on financial security, personal values, and material possessions. This period encourages you to take pride in your achievements and invest in things that bring you joy and satisfaction. You may feel more inclined to pursue financial goals that align with your sense of self-worth. Use this time to reflect on what truly matters to you and ensure that your financial decisions reflect your values.

AUGUST

Mon	Tue	Wed	Thu	Fri	Sat	Sun
					1	2
3	4	5	6	7	8	9
10	11	12	13	14	15	16
17	18	19	20	21	22	23
24	25	26	27	28	29	30
31						

NEW MOON

_____

_____

_____

_____

_____

_____

_____

_____

_____

_____

_____

_____

_____

_____

_____

_____

_____

_____

_____

_____

STURGEON MOON

31 Friday

The Pisces Moon encourages empathy and understanding in your interactions with others. It's a time to practice kindness, forgiveness, and unconditional love, fostering harmonious relationships and emotional healing. Embrace moments of empathy and connection, and allow yourself to be guided by the gentle currents of the Piscean energies. Open your heart to compassion and kindness, fostering deeper connections and a sense of unity with those around you.

1 Saturday

The Sun in Leo in the second house enhances your ability to manage your resources with pride and determination. You're likely to be more assertive in pursuing opportunities and more willing to invest in what brings you happiness. This influence can bring about a period of economic growth as you focus on building wealth and achieving your material goals. By staying true to your values and prioritizing your financial well-being, you can create an abundant life.

2 Sunday

Today's lunar ingress into Aries invites you to embrace a spirit of initiative, courage, and determination. Trust in your instincts, take decisive action toward your goals and embrace the dynamic energy of the Aries Moon to propel you on your path with enthusiasm and vitality. Embrace the opportunities for growth, self-discovery, and empowerment that arise during this energetic and action-driven lunar phase, and embrace the challenges as stepping stones to your success.

AUGUST

3 Monday

During today's astrological energies, your mind is buzzing with insights, sudden realizations, and flashes of inspiration. Use this heightened mental clarity and intuition to make bold decisions, pursue new interests, and communicate your thoughts and ideas with enthusiasm and conviction. Embrace the spirit of experimentation, stay open to unexpected opportunities, and trust in your ability to navigate change and innovation with ease.

4 Tuesday

When the Moon transitions into Taurus at 10:35 PM, a sense of stability, comfort, and grounded energy permeates the cosmic atmosphere, inviting you to slow down, savor the present moment, and connect with your senses. The Taurus Moon encourages you to focus on practical matters, material comforts, and nurturing your well-being. This lunar ingress brings a feeling of security and a desire to create a stable foundation for yourself and those around you.

5 Wednesday

During the Last Quarter Moon, you may feel a sense of culmination and closure regarding projects, goals, or emotional cycles that have been unfolding since the New Moon. It's a time to assess your achievements, acknowledge lessons learned, and release any attachments or obstacles that may be hindering your growth and progress. Reflect on your journey thus far and trust in the wisdom gained from your experiences.

6 Thursday

The Sun trine Saturn aspect supports perseverance, organization, and perseverance in pursuing your ambitions. It's a favorable time for setting realistic goals, implementing strategies for success, and taking practical steps toward achieving your aspirations. Embrace the supportive energy of this aspect to focus on tasks that require dedication, attention to detail, and a steady pace of progress. Trust in your ability to stay disciplined and committed to your goals.

7 Friday

Under the influence of the Gemini Moon, you may feel more mentally alert, friendly, and eager to explore diverse perspectives and interests. This lunar ingress invites you to embrace curiosity, engage in learning experiences, and connect with others through meaningful communication and interactions. Use this time to express your thoughts and ideas confidently, fostering open and engaging dialogues that promote mutual understanding and growth.

8 Saturday

Cosmic vibrations are aligning to encourage a deep sense of gratitude and appreciation for the beauty and abundance that surrounds you. As you attune to these celestial energies, you will find yourself awakening to the wonders of the present moment, cherishing the simple joys of life, and cultivating a profound sense of thankfulness that elevates your spirit and enhances your overall well-being, leading to a life filled with joy, fulfillment, and boundless positivity.

9 Sunday

Under the influence of the Cancer Moon, you may feel more attuned to your emotions, seeking comfort and support from loved ones and familiar environments. This lunar ingress invites you to nurture yourself and others, express empathy and compassion, and create a harmonious atmosphere that fosters emotional healing and connection. Use this time to engage in self-care practices that nourish your soul and strengthen your bonds.

10 Monday

Today's astrological aspects highlight themes of transformation, clarity, and purposeful action in relationships and personal growth. Embrace the intensity of Venus trine Pluto, navigate the nuances of Venus opposed Neptune with clarity and honesty, and harness the karmic energies of Mars sextile South Node and Mars trine North Node to align with your true path and create positive change in your life. Trust in the cosmic guidance and transformative energies to support you.

11 Tuesday

When Mars transitions into your sign, a shift in emotional assertiveness and drive occurs, emphasizing the importance of nurturing, protection, and sensitivity in pursuing goals and taking action. This Mars ingress encourages you to channel your energy into domestic matters, family connections, and emotional security, allowing you to assert yourself with empathy and care. It's a favorable time to prioritize self-care practices and nurture your emotional well-being.

12 Wednesday

Harness the energy of the New Moon to set intentions for growth, manifestation, and positive change. Utilize the Mercury-Uranus sextile to explore new possibilities, adapt to changes swiftly, and embrace the power of inspired thinking and communication. Trust in your intuition, embrace innovation, and seize the opportunities for growth and transformation that arise during this dynamic astrological period. Embrace the potential for unexpected breakthroughs.

13 Thursday

Embrace the practical and analytical energy of the Virgo Moon to tackle tasks with precision and efficiency, creating a sense of order and productivity in your day. Utilize the Mercury-Venus sextile to foster harmonious communication, deepen emotional connections, and cultivate mutual respect and understanding in your interactions. Trust in your ability to navigate daily responsibilities with grace and maintain harmonious relationships with those around you.

14 Friday

With Mercury in Leo transiting your second house, your approach to finances and material possessions becomes more confident and creative. This period encourages you to manage your resources with a focus on showcasing your talents and abilities. You may find yourself more interested in exploring innovative ways of earning and managing money. This is a time to channel your mental energy into building financial security through bold and imaginative strategies.

15 Saturday

Embrace the expansive and optimistic energy of the Mercury-Jupiter conjunction to pursue intellectual interests, share your wisdom, and embrace opportunities for personal and professional development. Utilize the Libra Moon's influence to foster cooperation, resolve conflicts peacefully, and create a sense of harmony in your environment. Trust in your ability to navigate conversations with wisdom and grace, promoting mutual understanding.

16 Sunday

Venus in Libra in the fourth house enhances your ability to manage family affairs with balance and diplomacy. You may feel more driven to achieve domestic goals through fair and harmonious efforts. It is a time to approach your home life with a thoughtful and balanced mindset. Your ability to create a well-ordered and peaceful environment can lead to significant harmony and emotional well-being. The focus on creating a balanced and harmonious home can enhance your life.

17 Monday

Mars forms a challenging square aspect with Neptune, creating a potential for confusion, low energy, and unclear motivations. This aspect may bring about challenges in asserting yourself effectively or taking decisive action. It's essential to stay grounded, clarify your intentions, and avoid getting swept away by unrealistic expectations or deceptive influences. Take this time to listen to your intuition, practice discernment, and proceed with caution in essential matters.

18 Tuesday

With Mars in Cancer transiting your first house, your drive and energy become more emotionally charged and intuitive. This period encourages you to pursue your goals with sensitivity and nurturing care. You may find yourself more protective of your interests and driven by emotional motivations. It is a time to channel your energy into personal projects that resonate deeply with your feelings and intuitions.

19 Wednesday

Embrace the energy of the First Quarter Moon to assess your progress, reflect on your intentions, and make any necessary adjustments to stay aligned with your goals. This lunar phase invites you to step into your power, take ownership of your journey, and embrace the opportunities for growth and transformation that come your way. Trust in your intuition, follow your heart, and take inspired action toward creating your desires. Use this time to set intentions and visualize success.

20 Thursday

With the Moon in Sagittarius, you may feel a strong desire for freedom, exploration, and personal growth. It is an excellent time to engage in activities that challenge you mentally, such as learning new skills, studying different philosophies, or planning future adventures. Embrace the opportunity to expand your horizons and embrace a more expansive view of the world and your place within it. Use this time to seek inspiration and broaden your perspective.

21 Friday

When Venus opposes Saturn at 8:42 AM, a sense of tension and restriction may arise in matters related to love, relationships, and finances. This aspect can bring about challenges in expressing affection, experiencing joy, or achieving harmony in partnerships. It's essential to be patient, realistic, and responsible in your interactions and commitments during this time. Use this aspect as an opportunity to strengthen your relationships by addressing any underlying issues.

22 Saturday

At 8:00 PM, the Sun opposes the North Node and conjoins the South Node, highlighting themes of karmic lessons, past patterns, and soul evolution. This aspect urges you to reflect on your past experiences, release outdated beliefs or behaviors, and align with your true purpose and destiny. Embrace the opportunity to let go of what no longer serves your growth and embrace new directions that align with your soul's journey.

23 Sunday

The universe is pulsating with the energy of transformation and renewal, signaling a time to let go of old patterns, beliefs, and habits that no longer serve your highest good. Embracing this period of metamorphosis allows you to shed your old skin and emerge anew with a revitalized sense of purpose, clarity, and direction. This cosmic reset brings forth the opportunity to reinvent yourself and step into a future brimming with potential and promise.

24 Monday

The cosmos is guiding you toward social activism and community involvement, inspiring you to make a positive impact in the world. This period is perfect for volunteering, advocating for causes you believe in, and working with others to create change. The celestial energies support your efforts to make a difference, guiding you toward opportunities that allow you to contribute meaningfully to society and inspire others to join you.

25 Tuesday

At 6:10 AM, Mercury opposes the North Node and conjuncts the South Node simultaneously, highlighting themes of communication, destiny, and life lessons. Mercury's opposition to the North Node may bring challenges or insights related to your path of growth and learning. It's essential to pay attention to communication patterns, beliefs, and information that may be hindering your progress or detouring you from your true purpose.

26 Wednesday

The universe is aligning to bring a surge of motivation and drive, encouraging you to pursue your passions and achieve your goals with unwavering determination. This period is perfect for setting ambitious targets, taking decisive action, and pushing through challenges with resilience and focus. The celestial energies support your journey toward success, guiding you to harness your inner strength and achieve remarkable accomplishments.

27 Thursday

The Sun's conjunction with Mercury enhances cognitive abilities, problem-solving skills, and mental agility. Utilize clear and effective communication to express yourself authentically and connect with others. Embrace the Pisces Moon's energy to cultivate compassion, empathy, and spiritual awareness, allowing yourself to navigate emotions with grace and understanding. Trust in your intuition and inner guidance as you navigate this dynamic astrological period.

28 Friday

Mercury forms a tense square aspect with Uranus, bringing about sudden insights, innovative ideas, and unexpected changes in communication. This aspect may stimulate mental restlessness, impulsive decisions, or disruptions in plans. Stay adaptable, think before reacting, and be open to new perspectives and unconventional solutions during this mentally stimulating transit. Embrace the opportunity to break free from limiting beliefs and explore new ways of thinking.

29 Saturday

The Moon's ingress into Aries at 10:37 PM marks a shift towards assertiveness, independence, and action-oriented energy. This lunar transit encourages you to embrace your inner drive, take initiative, and pursue your goals with enthusiasm and determination. Use this time to channel your passion, cultivate courage, and embark on new beginnings or projects that ignite your spirit. Embrace the dynamic energy of the Aries Moon to assert your needs and express yourself.

30 Sunday

With the Sun in Virgo transiting your third house, your focus is on communication, learning, and local connections. This period encourages you to hone your communication skills and pay attention to the finer details in your interactions. You may feel more inclined to engage in intellectual pursuits and enhance your knowledge base. Use this time to connect with your immediate environment and strengthen relationships with neighbors and siblings.

SEPTEMBER

Mon	Tue	Wed	Thu	Fri	Sat	Sun
	1	2	3	4	5	6
7	8	9	10	11	12	13
14	15	16	17	18	19	20
21	22	23	24	25	26	27
28	29	30				

New Moon

Corn/Harvest Moon

31 Monday

Embrace the supportive energy of the Jupiter-Saturn trine to create a solid foundation for your ambitions, make wise decisions based on experience and practicality, and seize opportunities for growth. Trust in your abilities, stay committed to your path, and utilize the positive influences of this aspect to achieve meaningful progress and lasting success. Embrace the harmonious alignment of Jupiter and Saturn to foster growth, build resilience, and manifest abundance.

1 Tuesday

At 5:58 AM, Mars forms a challenging square aspect with Saturn, highlighting potential frustrations, obstacles, and limitations in your actions and endeavors. This aspect may require patience, perseverance, and strategic planning to overcome hurdles and achieve your goals. Avoid impulsive actions, stay focused on long-term objectives, and use this energy to cultivate discipline and determination. Embrace the lessons of the Mars-Saturn square to build resilience.

2 Wednesday

Mercury in Virgo in the third house enhances your ability to communicate with precision and practicality. You may feel more driven to achieve intellectual goals through meticulous and well-organized efforts. Embrace this opportunity to refine your scholarly pursuits, creating connections that are both stimulating and productive. Your conversations can inspire and motivate others, making this an excellent time to engage in teaching, writing, or research projects.

3 Thursday

As the Moon enters Gemini, you may feel a heightened sense of curiosity and a desire for mental stimulation. Use this energy by seeking out new information, engaging in brainstorming sessions, and exploring creative ideas. Use the Gemini Moon's adaptable nature to multitask effectively, express yourself articulately, and connect with others through meaningful conversations. Embrace the mental agility and versatility of the Gemini Moon to engage in lively discussions.

4 Friday

As the Moon enters its Last Quarter, you may feel a sense of urgency to wrap up loose ends and make decisions that align with your long-term goals. Embrace this phase as an opportunity to evaluate your achievements, learn from challenges, and refine your plans for the future. Trust in your intuition and wisdom as you navigate this transitional period and prepare for the next phase of growth. Use the reflective energy of the Last Quarter Moon to gain valuable insights.

5 Saturday

The Moon in Cancer at 10:30 AM brings more emotional sensitivity. It raises your nurturing instincts and brings a focus on home and family matters. This lunar transit encourages you to prioritize self-care, nurture your emotional well-being, and create a supportive environment for yourself and your loved ones. Use this time to connect with your feelings, seek comfort in familiar surroundings, and foster deeper emotional connections with those you care about.

6 Sunday

Celestial energies foster a sense of gratitude and mindfulness, urging you to appreciate the present moment and cultivate a positive mindset that attracts abundance. It is a time for practicing gratitude, mindfulness, and living in the now, which can enhance your overall well-being and satisfaction with life. The universe supports your efforts to be present, guiding you toward a more fulfilling and contented existence that draws even more positivity your way.

7 Monday

The Moon's ingress into Leo at 12:49 PM invites you to embrace your inner leader, express your creativity, and bask in the warmth of recognition and admiration. Use this time to pursue activities that inspire you, engage in playful self-expression, and radiate positivity and enthusiasm in your interactions. Embrace the confident and vibrant energy of the Leo Moon to amplify your charisma, attract positive attention, and share your creative vision with others.

8 Tuesday

The Sun in Virgo in the third house enhances your ability to communicate with clarity and precision. You're likely to be more attentive to details in your conversations, making it an excellent time to engage in study or research. This influence can bring about a period of intellectual growth as you focus on learning and sharing knowledge. By prioritizing clear and effective communication, you can foster better understanding and cooperation in your relationships.

9 Wednesday

Embrace the grounded and analytical energy of the Moon's ingress into Virgo at 3:35 PM. This lunar transit encourages you to approach tasks with precision, attention to detail, and a focus on practicality. Use this time to organize your environment, streamline your routines, and address any areas of your life that require structure and order. Trust in your ability to tackle challenges methodically and achieve success through careful planning and disciplined action.

10 Thursday

The alignment of Venus trine the North Node and sextile the South Node at 2:07 AM signifies a harmonious balance between past experiences and future growth in matters of love, relationships, and personal values. This aspect encourages you to embrace positive connections and align your actions with your soul's evolutionary journey. Use this time to cultivate meaningful relationships, release outdated patterns, and move towards greater emotional fulfillment.

11 Friday

The Moon's ingress into Libra invites you to embrace the qualities of diplomacy, empathy, and partnership. This lunar shift encourages you to focus on creating harmony in your environment, resolving conflicts peacefully, and fostering a sense of unity and connection. Use this time to strengthen your relationships, express kindness and compassion, and find joy in shared experiences. Let the Libra Moon's influence guide you in finding common ground.

12 Saturday

Mercury's opposition to Neptune at 12:37 PM introduces dreamy and imaginative energy to communication but may also bring potential confusion or miscommunication. This aspect can inspire creativity, intuition, and spiritual insights, but it's essential to remain grounded and clarify any misunderstandings that may arise. Use this aspect to tap into your intuition, express yourself creatively, and explore the realms of imagination and fantasy.

13 Sunday

The Mercury trine Uranus aspect at 10:39 PM brings a surge of innovative thinking, intellectual stimulation, and the potential for sudden insights or breakthroughs. This harmonious alignment between Mercury, the planet of communication and intellect, and Uranus, the planet of innovation and change, enhances your mental agility, originality, and ability to think outside the box. It's a favorable time for brainstorming and experimenting with new ideas.

14 Monday

Use the combination of today's astrological influences to harness your inner strength, embrace transformational opportunities, and take decisive action. Trust in your ability to navigate challenges, stay focused on your priorities, and tap into your inner resilience and determination for success. Embrace the supportive energies of Scorpio, Capricorn, the Sun, and Mars to create a balanced approach to achieving your objectives and manifesting positive changes.

15 Tuesday

The Venus square Pluto aspect at 2:33 PM brings intensity, passion, and potential challenges in relationships and financial matters. This aspect may highlight power struggles, control issues, or deep-seated emotional dynamics that need to be addressed and transformed. It's essential to navigate this influence with honesty, integrity, and a willingness to confront underlying issues for healing and growth. Use this time to delve into the depths of your emotions and embrace vulnerability.

16 Wednesday

The Sagittarius Moon fosters a sense of optimism, growth, and a boundless thirst for knowledge, inviting you to focus on the abundance of opportunities that surround you and to expand your perspective on life. It's a highly favorable time for seeking out new experiences, gaining wisdom through exploration and learning, and connecting authentically with like-minded individuals who share your passions and values. Trust in the innate wisdom of your intuition.

17 Thursday

With Venus in Scorpio transiting your fifth house, your approach to creativity, romance, and recreation becomes more intense and transformative. This period encourages you to focus on expressing your passions and desires with depth and authenticity. You may find yourself drawn to intense romantic experiences and creative pursuits that uncover hidden aspects of your personality. It is a time to embrace your inner fire and allow your true self to shine.

18 Friday

As Mercury opposes Saturn at 6 AM, a complex interplay of communication styles and hierarchical dynamics may surface, prompting you to navigate interactions with tact, diplomacy, and a keen awareness of power dynamics. This celestial alignment underscores the significance of clear and structured communication, emphasizing the need for patience, empathy, and a willingness to listen and understand differing perspectives.

19 Saturday

Today's astrological influence of the Moon in Capricorn inspires you to embody qualities of resilience, determination, and practicality in your journey toward personal and professional fulfillment. Stay grounded in your approach to life, trust in your ability to overcome obstacles, and maintain a steadfast focus on your long-term goals. It is a time to align your actions with your vision, harness the supportive energies of the cosmos, and take decisive steps forward.

20 Sunday

Mercury in Libra in the fourth house enhances your ability to manage family communications with a sense of balance and fairness. You may feel more driven to achieve household goals through harmonious and well-thought-out efforts. Embrace this opportunity to refine your family dynamics, creating a harmonious household. Your problem-solving skills can help resolve domestic issues effectively, fostering a supportive and cooperative atmosphere at home.

SEPTEMBER

21 Monday

Under the influence of the Aquarius Moon, you may feel inspired to break free from conventions, explore unconventional ideas, and contribute to collective causes that promote progress and social change. This lunar ingress invites you to tap into your creativity, originality, and humanitarian spirit as you seek new ways to make a positive impact in the world. It's a time to envision a brighter future and take practical steps toward manifesting your vision.

22 Tuesday

During the September Equinox at 8:06 PM, the cosmos align in a delicate balance, marking a pivotal moment of transition and equilibrium between day and night. This celestial event heralds a shift in seasons, inviting reflection on balance, harmony, and the cyclical nature of life's rhythms. It's a time to honor the interplay of light and darkness, embracing the lessons of equilibrium and renewal that Equinox brings. As the Earth tilts, find solace in the promise of new beginnings.

23 Wednesday

As the Pisces Moon's gentle energy envelops you, you're encouraged to embrace moments of solitude, reflection, and spiritual contemplation. This lunar phase supports inner healing, emotional release, and a sense of oneness with the universe. Allow yourself to surrender to the flow of life, trust in the wisdom of your intuition, and let your imagination soar to new heights. Take this time to explore your dreams, meditate, and connect with your innermost desires.

24 Thursday

The universe is aligning to bring transformative experiences into your life, urging you to embrace change and let go of what no longer serves you. This period is perfect for decluttering your physical space, releasing past traumas, and welcoming new beginnings with an open heart and mind. The celestial energies support your transformation, helping you to shed old layers and emerge more robust and resilient. Embrace the changes ahead with courage and optimism.

25 Friday

The Sun's opposition to Neptune serves as a reminder to stay grounded, discerning, and aligned with your truth as you navigate the realms of imagination, intuition, and spiritual growth. Embrace the insights and inspirations that arise while remaining anchored in the present moment and honoring the wisdom of your inner guidance. Trust in the unfolding journey of self-discovery and spiritual evolution, knowing that clarity and understanding will guide you.

26 Saturday

As the Sun's harmonious trine with Pluto empowers transformation and the Moon's ingress into Aries sparks initiative, the Full Moon serves as a potent catalyst for personal and relational growth. Use this cosmic alignment to release what no longer serves you, embrace your inner power, and align your actions with your deepest desires and values. Trust in the transformative energies at play, and allow yourself to step into your full potential with confidence and authenticity.

27 Sunday

When Mars boldly transitions into Leo at 10:54 PM, the cosmic energies take on a fiery and bold tone, igniting passion, creativity, and a desire for self-expression. The Mars ingress into Leo infuses you with courage, confidence, and a strong sense of individuality, encouraging you to pursue your goals with enthusiasm and charisma. This energetic shift inspires you to embrace your inner fire, step into leadership roles, and express your unique talents with flair and conviction.

OCTOBER

Mon	Tue	Wed	Thu	Fri	Sat	Sun
			1	2	3	4
5	6	7	8	9	10	11
12	13	14	15	16	17	18
19	20	21	22	23	24	25
26	27	28	29	30	31	

NEW MOON

HUNTERS MOON

28 Monday

The combination of the Taurus Moon and the Sun trine Uranus offers a harmonious blend of stability and innovation. Embrace the pleasures of the moment while remaining open to new ideas and unexpected opportunities for growth. Trust in the natural flow, enjoy the beauty that surrounds you and be open to the magic of serendipity and positive change. Allow yourself to find the balance between comfort and exploration, and let the day unfold with grace.

29 Tuesday

The sextile between Mercury and the South Node invites you to reflect on the past, integrate valuable lessons, and release outdated thought patterns or communication habits. It's a favorable time for self-reflection, journaling, and inner dialogue that helps you gain insights into your subconscious mind and past experiences. Embrace this opportunity to clear mental clutter, release limiting beliefs, and communicate with greater clarity and authenticity.

30 Wednesday

At 1:26 PM, the Moon enters Gemini, infusing the atmosphere with curiosity, adaptability, and a desire for mental stimulation. The Gemini Moon's influence encourages you to embrace versatility, communicate with clarity and agility, and engage in diverse activities that stimulate your intellect. This lunar ingress sparks a sense of curiosity and a thirst for knowledge, making it an excellent time for learning, networking, and exploring new ideas and perspectives.

1 Thursday

The Sun in Libra in the fourth house enhances your ability to manage household matters with grace and fairness. You're likely to be more focused on creating a harmonious home, making it an excellent time to address domestic concerns and improve your living space. This influence can bring about a period of positive change in your home as you prioritize balance and harmony. By paying attention to the needs of your family and home, you can create a more supportive life.

OCTOBER

2 Friday

As the Moon gracefully transitions into your sign at 3:54 PM, the cosmic tone shifts towards emotional sensitivity, nurturing, and a focus on home and family. The Cancer Moon encourages you to prioritize self-care, connect with your emotions, and create a sense of comfort and security in your surroundings. It's a favorable time for nurturing relationships, expressing your feelings, and finding solace in familiar and nurturing environments.

3 Saturday

Today's astrological influences highlight themes of introspection, transformation, and release. Embrace the Venus retrograde period as an opportunity for inner growth and healing in matters of love and self-worth. Navigate the Mars-Pluto opposition with mindfulness and a focus on constructive communication and conflict resolution. Use the energy of the Last Quarter Moon to release the old and make way for new beginnings and positive changes in your life.

4 Sunday

Overall, today's astrological influences encourage a balance between responsibility and self-expression. Embrace the lessons of the Sun-Saturn opposition by staying committed to your goals and duties while also allowing the Leo Moon to inspire confidence, creativity, and a joyful approach to life. Find ways to express yourself authentically, overcome challenges with determination, and celebrate your achievements along the way.

5 Monday

With Mars in Leo transiting your second house, your approach to finances and material possessions becomes more driven by a desire for luxury and recognition. This period encourages you to focus on generating income and managing your assets with a confident and assertive attitude. You find yourself more willing to invest in what brings you joy and enhances your sense of self-worth. This is a time to channel your energy into building financial stability through bold strategies.

6 Tuesday

Later in the evening, at 10:52 PM, the Moon transitions into Virgo, ushering in a period of practicality, organization, and attention to detail. The Virgo Moon encourages you to focus on productivity, health, and daily routines. It's a favorable time for analyzing situations, making improvements, and taking care of practical tasks. Use this lunar phase to create order in your life, prioritize self-care, and attend to responsibilities with efficiency and precision.

7 Wednesday

Enjoy the dynamic and electric energy of the Mars sextile Uranus aspect as a catalyst for personal and collective growth. Trust in your instincts, be open to new experiences, and harness the power of innovation and creativity to propel you forward on your path. Use this cosmic alignment to break through limitations, embrace spontaneity, and ignite your inner fire for exciting new beginnings. Allow the synergy between Mars and Uranus to inspire you to take bold leaps.

8 Thursday

Celestial influences highlight the importance of mindfulness and mental well-being. Incorporate meditation, deep breathing exercises, and mindfulness practices into your daily routine to enhance your mental clarity and emotional balance. The universe supports your journey toward inner peace, helping you manage stress and improve your overall well-being. Trust the cosmic energy to guide you toward a state of mental and emotional harmony.

9 Friday

Overall, the Moon's ingress into Libra invites you to cultivate qualities of diplomacy, balance, and appreciation for beauty and harmony. Strive to create harmonious relationships, prioritize effective communication, and find ways to enhance the aesthetics of your surroundings. Trust in the power of cooperation and mutual understanding to create positive outcomes and foster a sense of unity and connection during this lunar transition.

10 Saturday

Venus squares Mars at 5:32 PM, creating a dynamic tension between love, desire, and assertiveness. This aspect may bring conflicts or challenges in relationships, highlighting differences in values, needs, or desires between partners. It's essential to navigate this energy with diplomacy, patience, and open communication to find a harmonious resolution. Use this aspect as an opportunity to address any underlying issues and express your needs assertively.

11 Sunday

Overall, today's astrological influence of the Moon in Scorpio invites you to dive deep into your emotional world and embrace transformational experiences. Allow yourself to explore the shadows, confront fears, and tap into your inner wisdom. Trust in the process of growth and change, knowing that each step forward brings greater understanding and personal empowerment. Allow the Scorpio Moon's intensity to guide you toward more profound self-awareness.

12 Monday

The cosmos is igniting your curiosity for technology and innovation. It is an excellent time to explore new gadgets, software, and tech trends that can enhance your personal and professional life. Embrace the advancements in technology to streamline your tasks, improve productivity, and stay ahead of the curve. The universe supports your quest for knowledge in this ever-evolving field, guiding you toward cutting-edge solutions and opportunities.

13 Tuesday

Overall, today's astrological influence of the Moon in Sagittarius encourages you to embark on a journey of discovery and personal growth. Allow the spirit of curiosity and adventure to lead you as you navigate life's pathways with excitement and optimism. Trust in your resilience, stay adaptable, and view each experience as a stepping stone toward greater understanding and fulfillment, embracing the journey with an open heart and mind.

14 Wednesday

With the Sun in Libra transiting your fourth house, your focus is on home, family, and emotional foundations. This period encourages you to create a harmonious and balanced living environment. You may feel more inclined to improve your home space and strengthen family bonds, ensuring that your domestic life reflects your values. Use this time to cultivate a sense of peace and beauty in your home, creating a nurturing and supportive atmosphere.

15 Thursday

Later in the day, at 11:36 PM, Pluto turns direct, marking a significant shift in the cosmic energy. Pluto's direct motion intensifies transformational energies, inviting you to release what no longer serves your growth and embrace profound changes. This planetary shift empowers you to confront deep-seated patterns, reclaim personal power, and undergo inner rebirth, allowing you to step into your authenticity and potential.

16 Friday

The combination of the Mars-Saturn trine and the Moon's ingress into Capricorn creates a powerful synergy for taking disciplined action, achieving goals, and building a solid foundation for future success. Trust in your abilities, stay focused on your priorities and use this time to implement practical strategies that lead to tangible results, knowing that your hard work and perseverance will pay off in the long run and contribute to your personal and professional growth.

17 Saturday

Mercury in Scorpio in the fifth house enhances your ability to channel your creative energies into intense and transformative endeavors. You may feel more driven to achieve artistic and romantic goals through focused and well-organized efforts. Embrace this opportunity to refine your creative and romantic life, creating experiences that are both stimulating and fulfilling. Your passionate approach can attract romantic interests and inspire artistic collaborations.

18 Sunday

The combination of the First Quarter Moon and the Moon's ingress into Aquarius encourages you to take proactive steps toward your goals while also fostering a sense of community and cooperation. Trust in your abilities, stay open to new perspectives and leverage the supportive energies to make progress both personally and collectively, knowing that your contributions have the potential to create positive change and inspire others.

19 Monday

The stars are aligning to inspire a sense of adventure and exploration in your life. Now is the perfect time to plan a trip, explore new destinations, and immerse yourself in different cultures. The universe supports your desire for new experiences, bringing excitement and growth to your journey. Allow the cosmic energy to guide you on an adventure that broadens your horizons, enriches your soul, and creates unforgettable memories.

20 Tuesday

The Venus-Pluto square encourages you to explore your deepest desires and fears related to love, intimacy, and financial security. It's a time for introspection and transformation, allowing you to confront any unresolved issues and make empowered choices that align with your values and priorities. Trust in your ability to navigate complexities and seek support if needed to facilitate healing, embracing this period as an opportunity for personal and relational evolution.

21 Wednesday

The Sun's sextile with the South Node at 6:34 AM invites reflection on past experiences, lessons learned, and karmic patterns that may need addressing. This aspect encourages you to integrate wisdom from the past while also embracing new opportunities for growth and transformation. Take time to honor your journey, release what no longer serves your highest good, and embrace the potential for positive change and renewal.

22 Thursday

Celestial forces are inspiring you to pursue new knowledge and expand your intellectual horizons. Enroll in courses, attend seminars, or dive into books and resources that ignite your curiosity. The universe supports your quest for learning, opening doors to new opportunities and broadening your understanding of the world. Embrace this period of intellectual growth to enrich your mind and enhance your personal and professional life.

23 Friday

The combination of the Sun's ingress into Scorpio, the Moon's ingress into Aries, and the Sun's conjunction with Venus in Scorpio creates a dynamic and transformative energy. Embrace the intensity of this time, trust in your inner strength and passion, and allow yourself to pursue your desires with authenticity and courage. Use this potent cosmic alignment to embark on a journey of self-discovery, assert your individuality, and cultivate meaningful connections.

24 Saturday

Mercury retrograde can offer opportunities for reconnecting with old friends, revisiting past interests, and gaining new insights from revisiting familiar experiences. Embrace the retrograde energy as a chance to learn from the past, gain clarity on your path forward, and refine your communication style for more effective interactions. Take this time to reconnect with people from your past who may offer valuable insights or support during this reflective period.

25 Sunday

As Venus gracefully enters Libra at 5:04 AM, it brings a wave of harmony, balance, and a renewed focus on relationships and aesthetics. This celestial shift invites you to appreciate beauty in all its forms, seek harmonious connections, and prioritize fairness and diplomacy in your interactions with others. Embrace this time as an opportunity to infuse your life with elegance, cultivate meaningful partnerships, and foster a sense of equilibrium and mutual understanding.

26 Monday

As the Full Moon graces the sky at 12:12 AM, it signals a time of culmination, heightened emotions, and the potential for clarity and release. This lunar phase invites you to reflect on your achievements, celebrate the progress made, and acknowledge any feelings that surface with compassion and understanding. Embrace the Full Moon's illuminating energy as a catalyst for closure, letting go of what no longer serves your growth, and setting intentions for the future.

27 Tuesday

At 9:02 PM, the Moon gracefully transitions into Gemini, ushering in a period of curiosity, versatility, and intellectual stimulation. This lunar ingress invites you to embrace a more adaptable and communicative approach to life, explore new ideas, and engage in meaningful conversations that spark your curiosity and expand your horizons. Embrace the airy energy of Gemini as it encourages you to be open to new experiences and connect with others.

28 Wednesday

With Jupiter in Leo transiting your second house, your focus is on financial growth, personal values, and material abundance. This period encourages you to approach your finances with a generous and expansive mindset, seeking ways to increase your wealth and resources. You may feel more inclined to invest in your talents and pursue opportunities that align with your values. Use this time to build a solid financial foundation and attract prosperity.

29 Thursday

Embrace the nurturing energy of Cancer as you focus on creating a sense of emotional security, fostering deeper connections, and honoring your feelings. This lunar transit encourages you to reflect on your roots, both emotionally and physically, and find comfort in familiar environments and routines. Allow yourself to be guided by intuition and empathy as you navigate the ebb and flow of emotions during this tender and reflective time.

NOVEMBER

Mon	Tue	Wed	Thu	Fri	Sat	Sun
						1
2	3	4	5	6	7	8
9	10	11	12	13	14	15
16	17	18	19	20	21	22
23	24	25	26	27	28	29
30						

143

NEW MOON

Beaver Moon

30 Friday

The harmonious aspects between Venus and the lunar nodes bring a blend of fate and choice in relationships and creative ventures. Embrace the positive influences that support your journey and alignment with your life's purpose, letting go of outdated beliefs or attachments that hinder your progress. Trust in the cosmic flow of opportunities and follow your heart's guidance as you navigate these celestial energies with grace and intention.

31 Saturday

With the Sun in Scorpio transiting your fifth house, your focus is on creativity, romance, and self-expression. This period encourages you to infuse your creative endeavors with passion and intensity, seeking deeper meaning in your pursuits. You may feel more inclined to explore transformative experiences in love and leisure. Use this time to engage in activities that allow you to express your true self and explore new dimensions of creativity.

1 Sunday

As the day progresses, at 3:29 PM, the Moon reaches its last Quarter phase, marking a pivotal moment for reflection, release, and preparation for new beginnings. This lunar phase encourages you to take stock of your journey, let go of what no longer serves your growth, and create space for fresh opportunities and transformative experiences in the upcoming lunar cycle, fostering a sense of renewal, empowerment, and readiness for positive change.

2 Monday

The stars are aligning to bring you an impressive opportunity, marking the start of an engaging and bustling chapter ahead. The fruitful outcomes you pursue now will lead to promising prospects and abundant growth. This time is rich with promise and prosperity, offering pathways to advance and hone your skills. Embrace your talents, as they will draw dividends and illuminate a journey of personal and professional evolution. A new vision is taking shape.

3 Tuesday

At 3:28 AM, the Moon transitions gracefully into Virgo, ushering in a period of practicality, organization, and a meticulous focus on details. This lunar ingress encourages you to approach tasks with efficiency, prioritize your responsibilities, and strive for excellence in your daily routines and endeavors, fostering a sense of order and productivity in your life. Embrace this time to create structured plans, implement systems that support your goals, and pay attention to the little things.

4 Wednesday

As the Sun aligns with Mercury in conjunction, tap into your mental acuity, articulate your thoughts clearly, and engage in conversations that foster understanding and collaboration. Utilize this alignment to clarify your goals, express your ideas with confidence, and make decisions that align with your vision and aspirations, leveraging your intellect and communication skills for success and growth. Allow this alignment to enhance your communication abilities.

5 Thursday

The Libra Moon encourages you to focus on aesthetics, beauty, and creating a harmonious environment. It's a favorable time for artistic endeavors, decorating your space, or engaging in activities that promote balance and serenity. Embrace the beauty around you and find inspiration in creating spaces that uplift and soothe the soul. Allow yourself to appreciate the artistry in your surroundings and infuse your environment with elements that bring joy and harmony.

6 Friday

The Sun in Scorpio in the fifth house enhances your ability to approach creative projects and romantic relationships with depth and passion. You're likely to be more focused on expressing your authentic self and exploring new forms of artistic expression. This influence can bring about romantic transformation as you delve into your passions and seek meaningful connections. By embracing your creative and romantic desires with intensity, you can experience greater fulfillment.

7 Saturday

Today's astrological influence of the Moon in Scorpio encourages you to dive deep into your emotional landscape, embrace authenticity, and embrace the transformative power of vulnerability. Use this time to explore your inner world, release what no longer serves you, and step into your power with confidence and authenticity. Trust in the process of transformation, knowing that every emotional experience is a stepping stone toward greater self-understanding.

8 Sunday

The universe is aligning to bring a sense of adventure and exploration into your life, urging you to step out of your comfort zone and embrace new experiences with open arms. This period is perfect for traveling, trying new activities, and expanding your horizons in every way possible. The celestial energies support your spirit of adventure, guiding you toward opportunities for growth, learning, and self-discovery.

9 Monday

Under the influence of the New Moon, you may feel a sense of renewal, optimism, and a desire to embark on new adventures. This energy of potential and possibility allows you to let go of the past and embrace the opportunities that lie ahead. Trust in the process of growth and transformation, knowing that each New Moon offers a chance for rebirth and renewal. Use this time to reflect on what you truly desire and set intentions that resonate with your heart's deepest desires.

10 Tuesday

Venus forms a harmonious sextile aspect with Mars, creating a harmonious and passionate energy that enhances romantic and creative endeavors. This planetary alignment encourages harmonious interactions, cooperation, and a balanced blend of assertiveness and diplomacy in relationships. Use this time to express your desires, pursue creative projects, and deepen connections with others through open communication and mutual respect.

11 Wednesday

With Saturn in Aries transiting your tenth house, your focus is on disciplined career advancement, public image, and long-term goals. This period encourages you to take a structured approach to your professional aspirations and public responsibilities. You may feel the need to redefine your career path and establish clear objectives. Use this time to build a solid foundation for your professional future. An ambitious approach to your career helps you achieve lasting success.

12 Thursday

Today's astrological influences of Jupiter opposing the North Node and conjuncting the South Node, along with the Moon in Capricorn, highlight the importance of balance, responsibility, and growth. Use this time to reflect on your journey, release what no longer serves you, and take disciplined action toward your goals and aspirations. Trust in your ability to navigate challenges with resilience, stay focused, and embrace the opportunities for advancement.

13 Friday

Today's influences of Mercury turning direct and Venus turning direct invite you to embrace clarity, harmony, and forward movement in your relationships and communications. Use this time to express yourself authentically, nurture meaningful connections, and align your actions with your values and intentions. Trust in the positive shifts taking place and move forward with confidence, knowing that the energies of growth, renewal, and love support you.

14 Saturday

With Mars conjunct South Node at the same time, you're confronted with energies from the past that could either hinder or support your progress. This conjunction urges you to reflect on past patterns of behavior, particularly those that no longer serve your highest good. It's a time to release old habits, beliefs, or attachments that keep you stuck in repetitive cycles, allowing you to embrace a more empowered and forward-looking mindset.

15 Sunday

When the Moon enters Aquarius, it brings a shift in your emotional energy. Aquarius, an air sign ruled by innovative Uranus, encourages you to take a detached and rational approach. This ingress invites you to embrace your uniqueness, step outside of your comfort zone, and explore unconventional ideas. It's a time when collective concerns may take precedence over your emotions, fostering a sense of community and humanitarianism.

NOVEMBER

16 Monday

When Mars aligns with Jupiter in conjunction at 1:23 AM, it signifies a potent fusion of energy and expansion. Mars, the planet of action, drive, and assertiveness, joining forces with Jupiter, the planet of growth, optimism, and abundance, creates a dynamic and ambitious atmosphere. This conjunction encourages boldness, enthusiasm, and a strong desire to achieve significant goals. You may feel a surge of motivation and a heightened sense of purpose.

17 Tuesday

At 8:13 AM, the Sun squares both the North Node and the South Node, creating a tense aspect that emphasizes karmic lessons and life path adjustments. The Sun Square North Node challenges you to step out of your comfort zone and align with your soul's purpose, while the Sun Square South Node urges you to release old patterns and beliefs that no longer serve your growth. This alignment may bring a sense of tension or conflict but also offers valuable insights.

18 Wednesday

When the Sun squares Jupiter at 4:38 AM, it signals a clash between expansive energy and the need for moderation. It highlights a period where optimism may need to be tempered with practicality and discernment. This aspect can bring a sense of overconfidence or exaggeration, prompting caution in decision-making and planning, reminding you to consider the bigger picture while staying grounded in reality and avoiding impulsive actions.

19 Thursday

When the Sun squares Mars at 12:49 PM, it ignites a dynamic and potentially confrontational energy, urging you to be mindful of impulsivity and assertiveness. This aspect can bring about tension, impatience, and a strong desire to assert oneself, emphasizing the need for patience and strategic planning in navigating challenges. It's crucial to approach situations with a calm and collected mindset to avoid unnecessary conflicts and ensure productive outcomes.

20 Friday

When the Moon ingresses into Aries at 12:52 AM, it heralds a shift towards assertiveness, action, and initiative. Aries, a fiery and energetic sign ruled by Mars, encourages boldness, courage, and a willingness to take on challenges head-on, igniting a spark of enthusiasm and a sense of adventure within you. This lunar transit invites you to embrace your inner warrior and approach tasks with renewed vigor and determination.

21 Saturday

Adventure and excitement figure prominently in the chapter ahead. It does see a social environment that connects you with others. It is an expressive, creative, and enriching time. New potential sweeps in with some significant changes in tow. It helps you kick off a path that sees life becoming energizing and active. You can get busy and embrace this social environment as it shines a light on connecting with friends.

22 Sunday

When the Sun ingresses into Sagittarius at 2:26 AM, it ushers in a period of exploration, optimism, and expansion. Sagittarius, ruled by Jupiter, encourages a broad perspective, a thirst for knowledge, and a sense of adventure. This solar transit invites you to embrace new experiences, seek higher truths, and cultivate a spirit of optimism and enthusiasm. It's a time to broaden your horizons, expand your beliefs, and embrace the diversity of life's experiences with an open mind.

23 Monday

When Venus forms a trine aspect with the North Node at 7:33 AM, it signifies a harmonious alignment between love, relationships, and your karmic path. This aspect brings opportunities for positive connections, soulmate encounters, and fulfilling partnerships that support your growth and evolution. It's a time to embrace love, harmony, and collaboration in your interactions with others. Use this harmonious energy to strengthen bonds and foster understanding.

24 Tuesday

The Full Moon occurs, illuminating the sky with its radiant energy. The Full Moon represents culmination, completion, and heightened emotions. It's a time of clarity, revelations, and manifestations, where intentions set during the New Moon come to fruition. Use this decisive lunar phase to celebrate achievements, release what no longer serves you, and align with your goals and desires. Reflect on how far you've come since the New Moon and acknowledge the growth.

25 Wednesday

The Sun forming a sextile with Pluto at 12:27 PM brings a harmonious alignment between personal power and transformation. This aspect encourages you to delve deep into your inner strengths, make positive changes, and embrace opportunities for growth and empowerment. It's a favorable time for self-discovery, healing, and stepping into your authenticity with confidence. Use this aspect to tap into your resilience and inner resources, allowing transformative shifts to occur naturally.

26 Thursday

The Moon in Cancer heightens your empathy, compassion, and desire for emotional closeness. It's a favorable time for self-care activities, spending time with family, and expressing your feelings openly. Allow yourself to tune into your intuition and honor your emotions during this lunar phase, as they provide valuable insights and guidance. Pay attention to your dreams and inner messages, as they may hold valuable information about your emotional needs and desires.

27 Friday

With the Sun in Sagittarius shining its light on your sixth house, your focus is on health, work, and daily routines. This period encourages you to approach your daily life with a sense of adventure, optimism, and enthusiasm. You may feel a strong desire to pursue new opportunities for improvement in your work or health habits. Use this time to adopt a positive and proactive approach to your daily routines, seeking out ways to enhance your well-being and productivity.

28 Saturday

When the Moon ingresses into Leo, it ushers in a period of heightened passion, creativity, and self-expression. Leo, ruled by the Sun, encourages confidence, playfulness, and a desire to shine. This lunar transit invites you to embrace your unique talents, showcase your personality, and engage in activities that bring joy and excitement. Take this opportunity to express yourself authentically, pursue creative endeavors, and bask in the spotlight of your radiant energy.

29 Sunday

When Uranus forms a trine aspect with Pluto at 6:23 AM, it signifies a harmonious alignment between revolutionary change and profound transformation. This aspect brings about a powerful synergy between innovation and regeneration, allowing for significant breakthroughs and positive shifts in various areas of life. It's a time for embracing change, releasing old patterns, and stepping into a new phase of growth and empowerment.

DECEMBER

Mon	Tue	Wed	Thu	Fri	Sat	Sun
	1	2	3	4	5	6
7	8	9	10	11	12	13
14	15	16	17	18	19	20
21	22	23	24	25	26	27
28	29	30	31			

NEW MOON

COLD MOON

30 Monday

When the Sun forms a trine aspect with Saturn, it brings a harmonious alignment between discipline, structure, and personal growth. This aspect encourages a sense of stability, responsibility, and long-term planning. It's a favorable time for making practical decisions, setting achievable goals, and laying solid foundations for future success. Use this harmonious energy to establish routines that support your ambitions and commit to taking steady steps towards your aspirations.

1 Tuesday

During the last quarter moon phase, you're urged to reflect on the progress made since the recent New Moon. It's a pivotal moment for you, a time for assessment and adjustment as you navigate the challenges and opportunities of the month. This phase encourages you to let go of what no longer serves you and to focus your energy on completing unfinished tasks or releasing habits that hinder your growth. It's a period of transition, preparing you for the upcoming lunar cycle.

2 Wednesday

As the Moon traverses through Libra, you're reminded of the importance of finding balance in all aspects of your life. Whether it's balancing your personal needs with the needs of others or finding equilibrium between work and leisure, this lunar transit encourages you to seek harmony and fairness in every endeavor. It's a time to cultivate inner peace and outer harmony, embracing the beauty of cooperation and collaboration as you journey through the lunar cycle.

3 Thursday

Mars in Virgo in the third house enhances your ability to communicate with clarity and precision. You may feel more driven to achieve intellectual goals through disciplined and detailed efforts. This is a time to approach your studies and interactions with a logical and systematic mindset, allowing your attention to detail to lead to deeper understanding and effective communication. Embrace this opportunity to refine your communication skills, creating impactful connections.

4 Friday

At 2:27 PM, you may encounter disruptive energy as Mars squares Uranus, igniting impulsiveness and rebellion. This aspect can bring sudden changes, unexpected events, or conflicts, challenging you to find innovative solutions to any obstacles that arise. It's essential to channel this dynamic energy constructively and avoid rash decisions or actions that could lead to unnecessary risks or conflicts, maintaining flexibility and adaptability in the face of change.

5 Saturday

Celestial influences are guiding you to embrace the power of authenticity and vulnerability, allowing you to show up fully and authentically in every aspect of your life. It is a time for honoring your truth, embracing your uniqueness, and sharing your gifts with the world without fear or reservation. The universe supports your journey of self-expression, guiding you toward opportunities that allow you to shine your light brightly and make a meaningful impact on others.

6 Sunday

You might find a sense of clarity as Mercury forms a trine with Saturn, grounding your thoughts and communication. This aspect supports practical thinking, making it an excellent time for planning, organizing, or engaging in tasks that require focus and attention to detail. Your words may carry weight and authority, facilitating productive conversations or negotiations with others. This alignment encourages you to approach your responsibilities with a disciplined mindset.

7 Monday

You might find stability and clarity as Mercury forms a trine with Saturn, grounding your thoughts and communication. This aspect supports practical thinking, making it an excellent time for planning, organizing, or engaging in tasks that require focus and attention to detail. Your words may carry weight and authority, facilitating productive conversations or negotiations with others. It's a favorable time to tackle complex projects or address any lingering responsibilities.

8 Tuesday

With Mercury's influence woven throughout the day's cosmic events, you are encouraged to embrace change, transformation, and the power of your thoughts and words. Stay open to the unexpected and trust in your intuition to guide you toward opportunities for growth and expansion. As you set your intentions under the New Moon's energy, remember the potential for profound transformation that lies within you, and allow yourself to step boldly into the future with confidence.

9 Wednesday

At 8:40 AM, brace yourself for potential conflicts or confrontations as Mercury squares Mars, igniting a surge of assertive energy in your communication. This aspect may lead to impulsive reactions or heated debates, so it's crucial to practice patience and diplomacy in your interactions. Avoid rushing into decisions or engaging in unnecessary arguments, and instead, channel this dynamic energy into productive activities that require focus and determination.

10 Thursday

The transition of Saturn from retrograde to direct motion often heralds a period of increased stability and accountability. During its retrograde phase, Saturn prompts you to reevaluate your responsibilities, boundaries, and long-term plans, urging you to confront any areas of weakness or stagnation. Now, as Saturn resumes its forward trajectory, you are called to implement the lessons learned and make tangible progress toward your objectives.

11 Friday

Under the influence of Mercury trine Saturn, your communication is characterized by clarity. You'll effortlessly articulate your thoughts with precision, making it easier to convey complex ideas or negotiate with confidence. This aspect favors structured dialogue and disciplined expression, allowing you to express your message effectively and garner the respect and attention of others. Take advantage of this auspicious alignment to engage in meaningful conversations.

12 Saturday

Neptune, the planet of dreams and illusions, shifts into direct motion after a period of retrograde. This celestial transition lifts the veil of confusion and uncertainty, bringing clarity and insight to your intuitive faculties. With Neptune moving forward, you're invited to trust your intuition, tap into your imagination, and pursue your most cherished dreams with renewed faith and conviction. Allow yourself to surrender to the flow of inspiration and creativity.

13 Sunday

The wheels are in motion to improve your circumstances. New possibilities trickle in at first, but curious options soon become a flood of potential that draws lighter energy into your life. It lets you focus on creating a journey that gives you a chance to elevate your abilities and grow your talents. You glide into a chapter of possibility that acts as a catalyst for change. It corresponds with developing endeavors as you embark on a mission to grow your life outwardly.

14 Monday

In this cosmic dance between the Sun and the Moon, you are invited to embrace the balance between destiny and intuition, action and surrender. Trust in the guidance of the North Node as it points you toward your true path while honoring the wisdom of the South Node as a source of strength and resilience. Allow the gentle embrace of Pisces to soften your heart and open you to the mysteries of the universe as you journey toward greater self-awareness.

15 Tuesday

Mercury in Sagittarius in the sixth house enhances your ability to manage your work and health with enthusiasm and insight. You may feel more driven to achieve professional and personal goals through strategic and well-organized efforts. Embrace this opportunity to transform your daily habits, creating a lifestyle that is both productive and fulfilling. Your strategic skills can lead to increased cooperation and effectiveness in your work environment.

16 Wednesday

Jupiter in Leo in the second house enhances your ability to attract wealth and improve your financial situation through creative and innovative means. You are likely to be more confident in your ability to generate income and secure your material needs. This influence can bring about a period of financial expansion and growth as you explore new ways to enhance your resources. By focusing on your strengths and remaining open to opportunities, you can create a prosperous life.

17 Thursday

With the Moon in Aries, you're encouraged to embrace your inner warrior and champion your ambitions. This lunar transit empowers you to take bold risks and pursue your dreams with courage and determination. Trust in your instincts and follow your inner guidance as you navigate the challenges and opportunities that arise. By tapping into the fiery energy of Aries, you can harness your resilience to overcome any obstacles and emerge victorious in your pursuits.

18 Friday

As the Sun trine Jupiter aspect unfolds, take a moment to bask in the glow of this auspicious alignment. Allow yourself to envision a future filled with possibility and abundance, and take inspired action towards manifesting your dreams. With the radiant energy of the Sun and the expansive influence of Jupiter by your side, there are no limits to what you can achieve. Embrace this moment as an invitation to step into your power and embrace the infinite potential that lies within you.

19 Saturday

As the Moon journeys through Taurus, you're supported in grounding your energy and reconnecting with your inner sense of worth and value. Take this opportunity to cultivate a deeper appreciation for your unique gifts. Trust in the stability and abundance of the universe to support you as you navigate life's ups and downs with grace and resilience. Embrace the nurturing energy of Taurus as you create a sense of security and fulfillment.

20 Sunday

At 12:31 PM, a significant alignment occurs as Mercury simultaneously forms a sextile with the North Node and a trine with the South Node. This rare synchronicity creates a potent cosmic portal for the integration of past wisdom and future insights into your present awareness. The North Node represents your soul's evolutionary path and the direction in which you're meant to grow, while the South Node symbolizes past patterns and experiences that you're releasing.

21 Monday

The December Solstice marks a significant astronomical event, signaling the beginning of winter in the Northern Hemisphere and summer in the Southern Hemisphere. This celestial phenomenon heralds the shortest day and longest night of the year, inviting you to turn inward and embrace the reflective energy of the season. It's a time for reflection, renewal, and setting intentions for the cycle ahead as you honor the rhythm of nature and the changing of the seasons.

22 Tuesday

Clear skies bring a wave of positivity to your social life, sparking insightful discussions and boosting your emotional well-being. Confidence will grow as you connect with new options that inspire personal growth. It is a time to embrace fun, connection, and kinship, with lively conversations leading to an engaging chapter of networking in a relaxed atmosphere. As you make notable progress toward your goals, freedom and expansion will beckon.

23 Wednesday

As evening approaches, the nurturing embrace of the Moon moves into the tender waters of your sign of Cancer, drawing you into the depths of your emotions and the sanctuary of your heart. Under this lunar influence, you are called to seek comfort and solace in the familiar embrace of home and family. It is a time to nurture your emotional well-being, tend to the needs of your loved ones, and cultivate a sense of security and belonging.

24 Thursday

Amidst the cosmic dance of stars that twinkle in the winter sky, the Christmas season emerges as a radiant beacon of light, guiding you toward moments of warmth, love, and togetherness. Embrace the celestial embrace by embracing the twinkling lights, the aroma of freshly baked cookies, and the laughter of loved ones gathered near, allowing the cosmic energies to infuse your spirit with the magic of the holiday season.

25 Friday

By late afternoon, the moon ingresses into Leo at 4:12 PM, infusing your emotional landscape with warmth, passion, and creativity. You'll find yourself craving self-expression and seeking opportunities to shine brightly in the spotlight. Embrace your inner fire and allow yourself to bask in the glow of self-confidence and authenticity. It is a time to indulge in activities that bring you joy and let your inner light radiate outward.

26 Saturday

As Mercury squares Neptune, you may feel a subtle shift in the currents of your consciousness. Neptune's ethereal influence can veil your perception, blurring the lines between reality and illusion. This aspect encourages you to tread gently, dear traveler, for the waters of Neptune's realm are deep and mysterious. Remember to approach communication with compassion and patience, recognizing the potential for misunderstandings to arise in the swirling mists of Neptune's domain.

27 Sunday

As you navigate through the practical energies of Virgo, remember to temper your perfectionist tendencies with a spirit of acceptance and humility. Embrace the beauty of imperfection and recognize that growth often arises from the messiness of life's journey. Trust in the wisdom of the universe as you work diligently towards your goals, knowing that every step forward is a testament to your resilience and strength.

28 Monday

As celestial forces converge, prepare for a vibrant period of growth and opportunity as life presents new paths to explore. By developing your social connections, you'll attract rewarding experiences and new friendships. This busy and exciting time will promote personal and professional progress. Supportive energies surround you, crafting a thriving environment where opportunities multiply, adding a delightful touch to your journey.

29 Tuesday

As Venus forms challenging squares with both the North Node and the South Node at 4:42 PM, you may feel a tug-of-war between the past and the future in matters of love, relationships, and values. These aspects urge you to confront any lingering karmic patterns or unresolved issues from the past that may be hindering your growth. Embrace this opportunity to release old attachments and step into alignment with your soul's evolutionary path.

30 Wednesday

At 2:00 PM, the moon enters its last quarter phase, signaling a time of reflection and release. This lunar phase encourages you to evaluate your progress and let go of anything that no longer serves your highest good. Embrace this opportunity to shed old habits, beliefs, or situations that are holding you back, making space for new growth and transformation in your life. Trust in the natural cycle of endings and beginnings, knowing that each phase of the moon brings valuable lessons

31 Thursday

Mercury forms a harmonious trine with Mars at 6:30 PM, amplifying your mental acuity and sharpening your communication skills. This aspect enhances your ability to think and speak with clarity and conviction, making it an ideal time for strategic planning, negotiations, and assertive expression. Trust in your intellect and intuition to guide you as you navigate through any challenges or opportunities that arise, knowing that you possess the inner resources to overcome obstacles.

2026 List of Astrological Events

The time zone is America Eastern Time, EST. The GMT offset is -5:00.

January

Thursday 1st
Sun sextile North Node 5:22 AM
Sun trine South Node at 5:22 AM
Mercury Square Neptune 8:33 AM
Mercury ingress Capricorn 4:12 PM
Friday 2nd
Venus sextile North Node 2:27 AM
Venus trine South Node 2:27 AM
Moon ingress Cancer 8:09 AM
Saturday 3rd
Full Moon 5:04 AM
Sunday 4th
Moon ingress Leo 8:43 AM
Tuesday 6th
Moon ingress Virgo 11:56 AM
Thursday 8th
Mercury sextile North Node 7:07 AM
Mercury trine South Node 7:07 AM
Moon ingress Libra 7:06 PM
Friday 9th
Venus opposed Jupiter 12:34 PM
Saturday 10th
Sun opposed Jupiter 3:42 AM
Mars opposed Jupiter at 9:25 AM
Moon last Quarter at 10:49 AM
Sunday 11th
Moon ingress Scorpio 5:55 AM
Tuesday 13th
Moon ingress Sagittarius 6:34 PM
Wednesday 14th
Mercury opposed Jupiter at 3:17 AM
Thursday 15th
Venus sextile Saturn 1:18 AM
Venus trine Uranus 10:22 AM
Friday 16th

Moon ingress Capricorn 6:47 AM
Saturday 17th
Venus sextile Neptune 3:33 AM
Sun sextile Saturn 5:41 AM
Venus ingress Aquarius 7:45 AM
Sun trine Uranus 11:58 AM
Sunday 18th
New Moon 2:53 PM
Moon ingress Aquarius 5:18 PM
Mercury sextile Saturn 11:09 PM
Monday 19th
Mercury trine Uranus 12:37 AM
Sun sextile Neptune 4:54 PM
Sun ingress Aquarius 8:47 PM
Tuesday 20th
Saturn sextile Uranus 12:18 AM
Mars trine Uranus 12:56 AM
Mars sextile Saturn 1:01 AM
Mercury sextile Neptune 9:34 AM
Mercury ingress Aquarius 11:42 AM
Wednesday 21st
Moon ingress Pisces 1:49 AM
Friday 23rd
Mars sextile Neptune 1:39 AM
Mars ingress Aquarius 4:20 AM
Moon ingress Aries 8:25 AM
Sunday 25th
Moon ingress Taurus 1:05 PM
Moon first Quarter at 11:48 PM
Monday 26th
Neptune ingress Aries 2:16 PM
Tuesday 27th
Moon ingress Gemini 3:55 PM
Thursday 29th
Moon ingress Cancer 5:31 PM
Saturday 31st
Moon ingress Leo 7:09 PM

February

Sunday 1st
Full Moon 5:10 PM
Monday 2nd
Moon ingress Virgo 10:21 PM
Tuesday 3rd
Uranus turns direct at 8:53 PM
Thursday 5th
Moon ingress Libra 4:32 AM
Mercury square Uranus 7:13 AM
Friday 6th
Mercury ingress Pisces 5:49 PM
Saturday 7th
Moon ingress Scorpio 2:13 PM
Sunday 8th
Venus Square Uranus 4:48 AM
Monday 9th
Moon last Quarter 7:44 AM
Tuesday 10th
Moon ingress Sagittarius 2:22 AM
Venus ingress Pisces 5:20 AM
Thursday 12th
Mercury opposed South Node 1:17 AM
Moon ingress Capricorn 2:44 PM
Friday 13th
Saturn ingress Aries 7:37 PM
Sunday 15th
Moon ingress Aquarius 1:16 AM

Monday 16th
Sun square Uranus 12:01 AM
Mercury trine Jupiter 4:28 PM
Tuesday 17th
New Moon 7:02 AM
Venus opposed South node 7:45 AM
Moon ingress Pisces 9:09 AM
Wednesday 18th
Sun ingress Pisces 10:54 AM
Thursday 19th
Moon ingress Aries 2:39 PM
Saturday 21st
Moon ingress Taurus 6:31 PM
Sunday 22nd
Venus trine Jupiter 3:01 PM
Monday 23rd
Moon ingress Gemini 9:29 PM
Tuesday 24th
Moon First Quarter 7:28 AM
Thursday 26th
Moon ingress Cancer 12:11 AM
Mercury turns retrograde at 1:47 AM
Friday 27th
Sun opposed South Node 7:32 AM
Mars square Uranus 11:20 AM
Saturday 28th
Moon ingress Leo 3:17 AM

March

Monday 2nd
Moon ingress Virgo 7:34 AM
Mars ingress Pisces 9:19 AM
Tuesday 3rd
Full Moon 6:39 AM
Wednesday 4th
Venus sextile Uranus 11:40 AM
Moon ingress Libra 1:56 PM
Thursday 5th
Sun trine Jupiter 12:13 PM
Friday 6th
Venus ingress Aries 5:47 AM
Moon ingress Scorpio 11:01 PM
Monday 9th
Mercury trine Jupiter 1:22 AM
Moon ingress Sagittarius 11:36 AM
Tuesday 10th
Venus sextile Pluto 2:52 AM
Jupiter turns direct at 11:36 PM
Wednesday 11th
Moon last Quarter at 5:39 AM
Thursday 12th
Moon ingress Capricorn 12:07 AM
Friday 13th
Mars opposed South Node 4:52 PM
Saturday 14th
Moon ingress Aquarius 11:13 AM
Monday 16th
Moon ingress Pisces 7:15 PM
Tuesday 17th
Mercury opposed South Node 5 PM
Wednesday 18th

Venus square Jupiter 12:08 PM
Sun sextile Uranus 4:20 PM
New Moon 9:24 PM
Thursday 19th
Moon ingress Aries 12:03 AM
Friday 20th
Vernal March Equinox 10:47 AM
Sun ingress Aries 10:48 AM
Mercury turns direct at 3:32 PM
Saturday 21st
Moon ingress Taurus 2:35 AM
Mars trine Jupiter 8 PM
Sunday 22nd
Mercury opposed South Node 8:49 PM
Monday 23rd
Moon ingress Gemini 4:18 AM
Wednesday 25th
Moon ingress Cancer 6:33 AM
Sun sextile Pluto 2:16 PM
Moon first Quarter at 3:18 PM
Friday 27th
Moon ingress Leo 10:10 AM
Saturday 28th
Saturn sextile Pluto 6:10 PM
Sunday 29th
Moon ingress Virgo 3:33 PM
Monday 30th
Venus ingress Taurus 12:02 PM
Tuesday 31st
Moon ingress Libra 10:51 PM

April

Wednesday 1st
Full Moon 10:13 PM
Friday 3rd
Mercury trine Jupiter 7:30 AM
Moon ingress Scorpio 8:11 AM
Venus square Pluto 6:38 PM
Sunday 5th
Sun square Jupiter 6:22 PM
Moon ingress Sagittarius 7:31 PM
Monday 6th
Venus sextile North Node 5:47 AM
Venus trine South Node 5:47 AM
Wednesday 8th
Moon ingress Capricorn 8:04 AM
Mars sextile Uranus 12:11 PM
Thursday 9th
Mars ingress Aries 3:39 PM
Friday 10th
Moon last Quarter 12:52 AM
Moon ingress Aquarius 7:55 PM
Monday 13th
Venus sextile Jupiter 4:20 AM
Moon ingress Pisces 4:55 AM
Tuesday 14th
Mercury sextile Uranus 1:11 PM
Mercury ingress Aries 11:23 PM
Wednesday 15th
Moon ingress Aries 10:03 AM
Thursday 16th
Mars sextile Pluto 2:55 PM
Friday 17th
New Moon 7:52 AM

Moon ingress Taurus 11:57 AM
Saturday 18th
Mercury sextile Pluto 4:35 PM
Sunday 19th
Moon ingress Gemini 12:17 PM
Sun ingress Taurus 9:41 PM
Tuesday 21st
Moon ingress Cancer 1:00 PM
Thursday 23rd
Moon ingress Leo 3:41 PM
Moon First Quarter 10:32 PM
Friday 24th
Venus ingress Gemini 12:05 AM
Saturday 25th
Sun square Pluto 12:32 PM
Moon ingress Virgo 9:04 PM
Uranus ingress Gemini 9:35 PM
Sunday 26th
Venus sextile Neptune at 1:42 PM
Mercury Square Jupiter 2:33 PM
Monday 27th
Sun sextile North Node at 9:19 AM
Sun trine South Node at 9:19 AM
Tuesday 28th
Moon ingress Libra 5:03 AM
Venus trine Pluto 12:39 PM
Wednesday 29th
Venus Square North Node at 9:19 PM
Venus Square South Node at 9:19 PM
Thursday 30th
Moon ingress Scorpio 3:02 PM

May

Friday 1st
Full Moon 1:24 PM
Venus sextile Saturn 2:45 PM
Saturday 2nd
Mercury ingress Taurus 10:57 PM
Sunday 3rd
Moon ingress Sagittarius 2:33 AM
Monday 4th
Mars square Jupiter 10:08 PM
Tuesday 5th
Moon ingress Capricorn 3:06 PM
Mercury square Pluto 6:08 PM
Wednesday 6th
Mercury sextile North Node 2:06 AM
Mercury South Node 2:06 AM
Pluto turns retrograde at 10:14 AM
Friday 8th
Moon ingress Aquarius 3:27 AM
Saturday 9th
Moon Last Quarter 5:11 PM
Sunday 10th
Moon ingress Pisces 1:39 PM
Sun sextile Jupiter 10:13 PM
Tuesday 12th
Moon ingress Aries 8:03 PM
Wednesday 13th
Mercury sextile Jupiter 12:43 AM
Thursday 14th
Moon ingress Taurus 10:31 PM
Saturday 16th New Moon 4:02 PM
Moon ingress Gemini 10:23 PM
Sunday 17th
Mercury ingress Gemini 6:27 AM

Monday 18th
Mars ingress Taurus 6:28 PM
Venus ingress Cancer 9:07 PM
Moon ingress Cancer 9:46 PM
Tuesday 19th
Mercury sextile Neptune 12:04 AM
Venus sextile Mars 1:37 AM
Mercury Square North Node 12 PM
Mercury Square South Node 12 PM
Mercury trine Pluto 6:52 PM
Wednesday 20th
Sun ingress Gemini 8:39 PM
Moon ingress Leo 10:48 PM
Friday 22nd
Venus square Neptune 2:31 AM
Mercury sextile Saturn 2:02 PM
Venus trine North node 5:55 PM
Venus sextile South node 5:55 PM
Saturday 23rd
Moon ingress Virgo 2:57 AM
Moon First Quarter 7:12 AM
Sunday 24th
Mars sextile North Node 9:56 PM
Mars trine South Node 9:56 PM
Sun sextile Neptune 10:22 PM
Monday 25th
Moon ingress Libra 10:34 AM
Sun square North node 3:22 PM
Sun square South node 3:22 PM
Tuesday 26th
Mars square Pluto 12:01 AM
Sun trine Pluto 11:52 AM
Wednesday 27th
Moon ingress Scorpio 8:52 PM
Thursday 28th
Venus square Saturn at 11:02 PM

Saturday 30th
Moon ingress Sagittarius 8:45 AM

Sunday 31st
Full Moon 4:46 AM

June

Monday 1st
Mercury ingress Cancer 7:57 AM
Moon ingress Capricorn 9:19 PM
Tuesday 2nd
Sun sextile Saturn 6:48 PM
Wednesday 3rd
Mercury trine North Node 7:39 AM
Mercury sextile South Node 7:39 AM
Mercury Square Neptune 8:17 PM
Thursday 4th
Moon ingress Aquarius 9:45 AM
Saturday 6th
Moon ingress Pisces 8:42 PM
Monday 8th
Moon last Quarter 6:01 AM
Tuesday 9th
Moon ingress Aries 4:33 AM
Wednesday 10th
Mercury square Saturn 1:37 AM
Thursday 11th
Moon ingress Taurus 8:27 AM
Friday 12th
Uranus square North Node 2:43 PM
Uranus square South Node 2:43 PM
Saturday 13th
Venus ingress Leo 6:49 AM
Moon ingress Gemini 9:06 AM
Sunday 14th
New Moon 10:55 PM
Monday 15th
Moon ingress Cancer 8:14 AM
Venus sex tile Uranus 6:52 PM

Tuesday 16th
Venus trine Neptune at 11:40 PM
Wednesday 17th
Moon ingress Leo 8:05 AM
Venus opposed to Pluto 4:38 PM
Friday 19th
Moon ingress Virgo 10:37 AM
Sunday 21st
June Solstice 4:25 AM
Sun ingress Cancer 4:27 AM
Moon ingress Libra 4:55 PM
Moon first Quarter at 5:56 PM
Tuesday 23rd
Sun trine North node 2:09 AM
Sun sextile South node 2:09 AM
Wednesday 24th
Moon ingress Scorpio 2:43 AM
Thursday 25th
Venus trine Saturn 8:01 AM
Sun square Neptune 6:38 PM
Friday 26th
Moon ingress Sagittarius 2:41 PM
Sunday 28th
Mars sextile Jupiter 12:50 AM
Mars ingress Gemini 3:33 PM
Monday 29th
Moon ingress Capricorn 3:18 AM
Mercury turns retrograde at 1:35 PM
full Moon 7:57 PM
Tuesday 30th
Mars square North node 1:31 AM
Mars square South node 1:31 AM
Jupiter ingress Leo 2:07 AM

July

Wednesday 1st
Moon ingress Aquarius 3:33 PM
Saturday 4th
Moon ingress Pisces 2:30 AM
Mars sextile Neptune 8:44 PM
Sunday 5th
Mars trine Pluto 9:06 AM
Monday 6th
Sun square Saturn 6:47 AM
Moon ingress Aries 11:07 AM
Tuesday 7th
Neptune turns retro at 7:40 AM
Moon last Quarter 3:30 PM
Wednesday 8th
Moon ingress Taurus 4:30 PM
Thursday 9th
Venus ingress Virgo 1:25 PM
Friday 10th
Venus opposed North Node 4:20 AM
Moon ingress Gemini 6:41 PM
Sunday 12th
Moon ingress Cancer 6:46 PM
Monday 13th
Venus Square Uranus 10:26 AM
Tuesday 14th
New Moon 5:44 AM
Moon ingress Leo 6:35 PM
Wednesday 15th
Uranus sextile Neptune 4:35 PM
Thursday 16th
Moon ingress Virgo 8:07 PM
Saturday 18th
Uranus trine Pluto 12:43 AM

Sunday 19th
Moon ingress Libra 12:57 AM
Mars sextile Saturn 2:10 PM
Monday 20th
Jupiter trine Neptune 3:23 AM
Jupiter opposed Pluto at 10:44 AM
Tuesday 21st
Moon First Quarter 7:06 AM
Jupiter sextile Uranus 7:10 AM
Moon ingress Scorpio 9:35 AM
Wednesday 22nd
Sun ingress Leo 3:16 PM
Thursday 23rd
Mercury turns direct at 6:58 PM
Sagittarius 9:07 PM
Friday 24th
Mercury sextile Venus 12:08 PM
Saturday 25th
Neptune sextile Pluto 1:25 AM
Sunday 26th
Moon ingress Capricorn 9:44 AM
Saturn turns retrograde at 3:29 PM
Nth Node ingress Aquarius 9:02 PM
South Node ingress Leo 9:02 PM
Monday 27th
Sun opposed Pluto at 2:55 AM
Sun trine Neptune 3:36 AM
Sun sextile Uranus 5:36 PM
Tuesday 28th
Moon ingress Aquarius 9:46 PM
Wednesday 29th
Venus square Mars 3:09 AM
Full Moon 10:36 AM
Friday 31st
Moon ingress Pisces 8:14 AM

August

Sunday 2nd
Moon ingress Aries 4:36 PM
Tuesday 4th
Moon ingress Taurus 10:35 PM
Wednesday 5th
Moon last Quarter at 10:22 PM
Thursday 6th
Venus ingress Libra 3:16 PM
Sun trine Saturn 10:44 PM
Friday 7th
Moon ingress Gemini 2:07 AM
Sunday 9th
Moon ingress Cancer 3:45 AM
Mercury ingress Leo 12:30 PM
Monday 10th
Venus trine Pluto 2:08 PM
Venus opposed Neptune 6:01 PM
Mars sextile South Node 11:38 PM
Mars trine North Node 11:38 PM
Tuesday 11th
Mars ingress Cancer 4:36 AM
Moon ingress Leo 4:38 AM
Mercury opposed Pluto 9:20 PM
Mercury trine Neptune at 11:40 PM
Venus trine Uranus at 11:45 PM
Wednesday 12th
New Moon 1:37 PM
Mercury sextile Uranus 4:49 PM
Thursday 13th
Moon ingress Virgo 6:18 AM
Mercury sextile Venus 12:25 PM
Saturday 15th
Mercury conjunct Jupiter 7:23 AM
Moon ingress Libra 10:20 AM

Monday 17th
Mars square Neptune 5:52 AM
Mercury trine Saturn 11:27 AM
Venus sextile Jupiter 12:15 PM
Moon ingress Scorpio 5:46 PM
Wednesday 19th
Moon First Quarter at 10:47 PM
Thursday 20th
Moon ingress Sagittarius 4:30 AM
Friday 21st
Venus opposed Saturn 8:42 AM
Saturday 22nd
Moon ingress Capricorn 4:59 PM
Sun opposed North Node 8 PM
Sun conjunct South Node 8 PM
Sun ingress Virgo 10:22 PM
Tuesday 25th
Moon ingress Aquarius 5:01 AM
Mercury opposed North Node 6:10 AM
Mercury conjunct South Node 6:10 AM
Mercury ingress Virgo 7:06 AM
Thursday 27th
Sun conjunct Mercury 1:03 PM
Moon ingress Pisces 3:03 PM
Friday 28th
Full Moon 12:19 AM
Mercury square Uranus 3:24 AM
Sun square Uranus 6:18 PM
Saturday 29th
Moon ingress Aries 10:37 PM
Monday 31st
Jupiter trine Saturn 6:17 PM

September

Tuesday 1st
Moon ingress Taurus 4:01 AM
Mars square Saturn at 5:58 AM
Mercury sextile Mars 9:20 AM
Thursday 3rd
Moon ingress Gemini 7:47 AM
Friday 4th
Moon Last Quarter 3:52 AM
Saturday 5th
Moon ingress Cancer 10:30 AM
Monday 7th
Moon ingress Leo 12:49 PM
Wednesday 9th
Moon ingress Virgo 3:35 PM
Thursday 10th
Venus trine North Node 2:07 AM
Venus sextile South Node 2:07 AM
Venus ingress Scorpio 4:12 AM
Mercury ingress Libra 12:22 PM
Uranus turns retrograde at 3:29 PM
New Moon 11:28 PM
Friday 11th
Moon ingress Libra 7:52 PM
Saturday 12th
Mercury trine Pluto 11:58 AM
Mercury opposed Neptune at 12:37 PM
Sunday 13th
Mercury trine Uranus 10:39 PM
Monday 14th
Moon ingress Scorpio 2:44 AM
Black Moon ingress Capricorn 1:37 PM
Sun sextile Mars 3:53 PM

Tuesday 15th
Venus square Pluto 2:33 PM
Neptune sextile Pluto 10:10 PM
Wednesday 16th
Moon ingress Sagittarius 12:41 PM
Friday 18th
Mercury opposed Saturn at 6 AM
Moon First Quarter 4:44 PM
Saturday 19th
Moon ingress Capricorn 12:55 AM
Monday 21st
Moon ingress Aquarius 1:14 PM
Mercury sextile Jupiter 6:50 PM
Tuesday 22nd
September Equinox 8:06 PM
Sun ingress Libra 8:08 PM
Wednesday 23rd
Moon ingress Pisces 11:23 PM
Friday 25th
Sun opposed Neptune 9:36 PM
Saturday 26th
Sun trine Pluto 1:34 AM
Moon ingress Aries 6:23 AM
Full Moon 12:50 PM
Sunday 27th
Mars ingress Leo 10:54 PM
Monday 28th
Moon ingress Taurus 10:40 AM
Sun trine Uranus 12:21 PM
Tuesday 29th
Mercury trine North Node 6:03 PM
Mercury sextile South Node 6:03 PM
Wednesday 30th
Mercury ingress Scorpio 7:47 AM
Moon ingress Gemini 1:26 P

October

Friday 2nd
Mercury square Mars 5:13 AM
Moon ingress Cancer 3:54 PM
Mercury square Pluto 4:42 PM
Mars trine Neptune 6:17 PM
Saturday 3rd
Venus turns retrograde at 3:14 AM
Mars opposed Pluto 6:38 AM
Moon Last Quarter 9:26 AM
Sunday 4th
Sun opposed Saturn 8:29 AM
Moon ingress Leo 6:54 PM
Tuesday 6th
Mercury conjunct Venus 8:10 PM
Moon ingress Virgo 10:52 PM
Wednesday 7th
Mars sextile Uranus 6:41 AM
Friday 9th
Moon ingress Libra 4:10 AM
Saturday 10th
new Moon 11:51 AM
Venus square Mars 5:32 PM
Sunday 11th
Moon ingress Scorpio 11:21 AM
Tuesday 13th
Moon ingress Sagittarius 8:59 PM
Thursday 15th
Sun sextile Jupiter 4:21 AM
Pluto turns direct at 11:36 PM
Friday 16th
Mars trine Saturn 4:32 AM

Moon ingress Capricorn 5:57 AM
Sunday 18th
Moon First Quarter 12:13 PM
Moon ingress Aquarius 9:40 PM
Tuesday 20th
Venus square Pluto at 2:57 AM
Wednesday 21st
Sun trine North Node 6:34 AM
Sun sextile South Node 6:34 AM
Moon ingress Pisces 8:35 AM
Friday 23rd
Sun ingress Scorpio 5:41 AM
Moon ingress Aries 5:53 PM
Sun conjunct Venus 11:44 PM
Saturday 24th
Mercury turns retrograde at 3:13 AM
Sunday 25th
Venus ingress Libra 5:04 AM
Moon ingress Taurus 7:34 PM
Monday 26th
Full Moon 12:12 AM
Sun square Pluto 8:11 AM
Tuesday 27th
Moon ingress Gemini 9:02 PM
Thursday 29th
Moon ingress Cancer 10:05 PM
Friday 30th
Mercury square Mars 1:23 PM
Venus trine North Node 6:13 PM
Venus sextile South Node 6:13 PM

November

Sunday 1st
Moon ingress Leo 12:18 AM
Moon last Quarter 3:29 PM
Tuesday 3rd
Moon ingress Virgo 3:28 AM
Wednesday 4th
Venus sextile Jupiter 5:28 AM
Sun conjunct Mercury 9:24 AM
Thursday 5th
Moon ingress Libra 9:38 AM
Saturday 7th
Moon ingress Scorpio 5:40 PM
Monday 9th
New Moon 2:03 AM
Tuesday 10th
Venus sextile Mars 1:45 AM
Moon ingress Sagittarius 3:36 AM
Thursday 12th
Jupiter opposed North Node 12:13 AM
Jupiter conjunct South Node 12:13 AM
Moon ingress Capricorn 3:27 PM
Friday 13th
Mercury turns direct at 10:54 AM
Venus turns direct at 7:28 PM
Saturday 14th
Mars opposed North Node 2:57 PM
Mars conjunct South Node 2:57 PM
Sunday 15th
Moon ingress Aquarius 4:24 AM
Monday 16th
Mars conjunct Jupiter at 1:23 AM

Tuesday 17th
Moon First Quarter 6:49 AM
Sun square North Node 8:13 AM
Sun square South Node 8:13 AM
Moon ingress Pisces 4:19 PM
Wednesday 18th
Sun square Jupiter 4:38 AM
Thursday 19th
Sun square Mars 12:49 PM
Friday 20th
Moon ingress Aries 12:52 AM
Sunday 22nd
Sun ingress Sagittarius 2:26 AM
Moon ingress Taurus 5:09 AM
Monday 23rd
Venus trine North Node 7:33 AM
Venus sextile South Node 7:33 AM
Sun trine Neptune 7:07 PM
Tuesday 24th
Moon ingress Gemini 6:09 AM
Full Moon 9:54 AM
Wednesday 25th
Sun sextile Pluto 12:27 PM
Sun opposed Uranus 5:41 PM
Mars ingress Virgo 6:45 PM
Thursday 26th
Moon ingress Cancer 5:51 AM
Saturday 28th
Moon ingress Leo 6:20 AM
Venus sex tile Jupiter 7:07 AM
Sunday 29th
Uranus trine Pluto 6:23 AM
Monday 30th
Sun trine Saturn 1:05 AM
Moon ingress Virgo 9:13 AM

December

Tuesday 1st
Moon last Quarter 1:09 AM
Mercury square North node 10:06 PM
Mercury square South node 10:06 PM
Wednesday 2nd
Moon ingress Libra 3:04 PM
Friday 4th
Mercury square Jupiter 2:02 AM
Venus ingress Scorpio 3:17 AM
Mars square Uranus 2:27 PM
Moon ingress Scorpio 11:35 PM
Sunday 5th
Mercury ingress Sagittarius 3:35 AM
Monday 7th
Mercury trine Neptune 5:15 AM
Moon ingress Sagittarius 10:06 AM
Tuesday 8th
Mercury opposed Uranus 5:29 AM
Mercury sextile Pluto 2:31 PM
New Moon 7:53 PM
Wednesday 9th
Mercury square Mars 8:40 AM
Venus square Pluto 1:38 PM
Moon ingress Capricorn 10:09 PM
Thursday 10th
Saturn turns direct at 7 PM
Friday 11th
Mercury trine Saturn 8:25 AM
Saturday 12th
Venus sextile Mars 4:16 a.m.
Moon ingress Aquarius 11:05 AM

Neptune turns direct at 6:11 PM
Jupiter turns retrograde at 7:47 PM
Monday 14th
Sun sextile North Node 3:59 AM
Sun trine South Node 3:59 AM
Moon ingress Pisces 11:35 PM
Thursday 17th
Moon First Quarter 12:43 AM
Moon ingress Aries 9:34 AM
Friday 18th
Sun trine Jupiter 4:21 PM
Saturday 19th
Moon ingress Taurus 3:29 PM
Sunday 20th
Mercury sextile North Node 12:31 PM
Mercury trine South Node 12:31 PM
Monday 21st
December Solstice 3:51 PM
Sun ingress Capricorn 3:54 PM
Moon ingress Gemini 5:27 PM
Wednesday 23rd
Sun square Neptune 6:37 AM
Mercury trine Jupiter 1:03 PM
Moon ingress Cancer 4:58 PM
Full Moon 8:29 PM
Friday 25th
Mercury ingress Capricorn 1:25 PM
Moon ingress Leo 4:12 PM
Saturday 26th
Mercury square Neptune 2:46 PM
Sunday 27th
Moon ingress Virgo 5:13 PM
Tuesday 29th
Venus square North Node 4:42 PM

Venus square South Node 4:42 PM
Sun square Saturn 6:27 PM
Moon ingress Libra 9:27 PM
Wednesday 30th
Moon last Quarter 2 PM

Mercury square Saturn 6:54 PM
Thursday 31st
Sun trine Mars 7:03 AM
Mercury trine Mars 6:30 PM

Astrology, Tarot & Horoscope Books.

Mystic Cat